Pelican Books
Anatomy of the Law

D1549777

Lon L. Fuller holds the Carter Professorship of
General Jurisprudence in the Harvard Law School.
He has frequently been called upon in the United
States to serve as an arbitrator in labour disputes.
Among his published works are many articles and
the following books: *The Law in Quest of Itself, The
Morality of Law, Legal Fictions* and a casebook
co-edited with Robert Braucher, *Basic Contract Law*.

Lon L. Fuller

Anatomy of the Law

Penguin Books

Penguin Books Ltd, Harmondsworth,
Middlesex, England
Penguin Books Australia Ltd, Ringwood,
Victoria, Australia

First published in U.S.A. by Frederick A. Praeger 1968
First published in Great Britain by Pall Mall Press 1968
Published in Pelican Books 1971
Copyright © Encyclopaedia Britannica, Inc., 1968

Made and printed in Great Britain by
Richard Clay (The Chaucer Press) Ltd,
Bungay, Suffolk
Set in Linotype Times

Contents

Part 1

Pervasive Problems of the Law

Law as a dimension of human life

To the thoughtful and sensitive citizen the law can present itself in a bewildering array of moods. It can appear as the highest achievement of civilization, liberating for creative use human resources otherwise dedicated to destruction. It can be seen as the foundation of human dignity and freedom, our best hope for a peaceful world. In man's capacity to perceive and legislate against his own defects we can discern his chief claim to stand clearly above the animal level. Philosophers of former ages have, indeed, not hesitated to see some kinship with the divine in man's ability to reorder his own faulty nature and, in effect, to re-create himself by the rule of reason.

A shift in mood and all this bright glitter surrounding the law can collapse into dust. Law then becomes man's badge of infamy, his confession of ineradicable perfidy. To say that man can reshape himself by rules is to confess that he is a creature who has to put a halter on himself before he can live safely with his fellows. If this is something no other animal can do, it is something no other animal needs to do, for mankind is the only species that chooses its own kind as its preferred prey. Viewing the law in this gloomy light, we may gladly share the dreams of Tolstoi and Marx that a future may come in which men can live simply and affectionately with one another and without the crutch of rules.

In its relation with other human sciences, the law can present a similar antithesis. It can be said that the law is the oldest and richest of the social sciences. Before there were psychologists, judges had to deal with problems of intent and responsibility, and their way of dealing with these problems seems to many even now to contain a deeper wisdom than that to be found in textbooks on psychology. Economists who have exhausted the resources of their own science turn to the law for insight into the nature of the institutional arrangements essential for a free economy. Philosophers find in the law a discipline lacking in their own sometimes errant studies – the discipline, namely, that comes of accepting the responsibility for rendering decisions by which men can shape their lives. The philosopher not yet turned king or judge can say of his profession:

We tread a higher ground, self-determined, universal. Our decisions do not have that unkind quality of irrevocability, and do not weave the same imprisoning web about us. If we are wrong, we have simply to change our minds.*

When the philosopher descends from this high plateau to share in the tasks of the judge and the legislator, he seems to be surrendering the freedom of his thought for a burdensome responsibility. Yet in this exchange he often acquires a new and liberating sense of direction.

Because the law throughout its history has been compelled to remain immersed in the stream of human life itself, inevitably the forms of its thought have become a part of the vocabulary of everyday living. The law has in fact made indispensable contributions to language. One thinks at once of such words as 'judgment', 'judicious', and 'just'. But the contributions are by no means always of so obvious a nature; the words 'average' and 'thing', for example, took their origin in a legal and legislative context. To have contributed the last word – understood by every child – may not seem a significant service until we notice the degree of abstraction involved in it and recall that every step toward abstract thought comes hard in the early history of language. The reader may recapture some of the significance of this particular step if he asks himself how, if he were a dictionary maker, he would define the word 'thing'.

In an opposing light, law can seem the emptiest of sciences. It is all means and no end, a science frightening in its adaptability, holding its rough engine ready to serve all comers who

* C. J. Vining, Valedictorian Dissertation, Harvard University, 11 June 1964.

can show the proper papers. The law has indeed been said to be the only human study having no distinctive ends of its own. Where its ends can be regarded as grounded in reason, and not brute expressions of political power, those ends must be derived not from the law itself but from ethics, sociology, and economics. If it is empty of ends, the law can hardly be said to be attractive in the means it employs. At their best these means represent measures designed to restore a condition of social health itself not a direct product of law. At their worst they involve the deliberate infliction of pain. Economics has been described as 'the dismal science'. But economics at least deals with the allocation of scarce goods, while the law deliberately apportions evils on a world already oversupplied with suffering.

When it is said that law represents the rule of reason, it is appropriate to ask what kind of reason is meant. Here again we encounter sharply contrasting views, though in this case neither branch of the antithesis is flattering to the law. For some, law is all intellect and no common sense. It defends with laboured paragraphs what the layman thinks he could explain in two sentences. It will not permit the witness in court to tell what he saw in the language of everyday life, but forces his description into the artificial forms of its own rationalizations. The witness genuinely eager to help the judge and jury finds himself stopped in mid sentence when he tries to tell what he knows in the terms that come naturally to him – when he uses, in other words, the only language in which he can be sure whether he is telling the truth. Over the whole proceeding hovers what Lord Coke proudly called 'the artificial reason of the law'. The legal profession as a whole, according to one of its critics, recruits its members by a kind of natural selection from among those temperamentally inclined toward 'over-thinking'.

At the opposite pole, law appears as a world of brute fiat, in which things are as they are because they have always been so, where it is more persuasive to argue that a rule has been applied for centuries than that it is sensible and just. Justice Holmes in a famous passage remarked that it is 'revolting to have no better reason for a rule of law than that so it was laid down in the time of Henry IV'. The implication of his remark was, of course, that this is precisely the kind of reason often relied upon by lawyers.

All of these divergent views see the law as cutting, in different directions, deeply into human life. All share a certain mood of earnest concern. Some respite from this mood may be gained by recalling the gay role played by the law in Gilbert and Sullivan. Their legal world is one of fancy and make-believe in which everyone knows the law, rotund chancellors embody it, husband and wife are one, while Equity belies its name and shirks its job by deeming that as done which ought to be done.

But any relief obtained by this shift of scenes is soon clouded when we reflect that the unhappy litigant whose fate depends on these flights of verbal fancy will see little to admire in their ingenuity. The layman would probably rather be found guilty of fraud, for he can then say the court was wrong, than be found guilty of 'constructive fraud', for he does not know what that means and he may doubt whether the court does either.

These, then, are the moods in which the law may appear to the man previously described as 'the thoughtful and sensitive citizen'. It is probably safe to say that most of mankind over most of its history has been a stranger to all of these moods. For the man in the street or in the field the most common response to the law is a gesture of helplessness and indifference. The law is like the weather. It is there, you adjust to it, but there is nothing you can do about it except to get under cover when its special kind of lightning strikes. Certainly it furnishes no special occasion for moralizing or philosophizing.

This mood is poignantly conveyed in the following passage from a report of the experiences of an American scholar who spent a year in the Soviet Union, mostly in visiting the law courts:

Like the cruel climate, sparse soil, and poor peasantry, courts and law seemed to be accepted as features of the landscape about which nothing can be done because higher powers have willed them. It has always been so ... when I asked specifically whether the courts were *spravedliviye* ('just'. or 'fair'), the answer was usually a shrug and an uncertain '*Da*'. A shrug because the question seemed strange to them. Ordinary Russians are passive about such things, considering the law neither good nor bad, but unavoidable – not for the likes of *them* to contemplate. This is to say, they very seldom think about the law. '*Shto podylaiyesh?* – What can you do about it?'

This (Eastern?) attitude implies that love of law as a positive good is not natural to Russians and indeed it was not spoken of admiringly, even by law students. It is no accident, as Soviet professors love to say, that law students and the Law Faculty have the (deserved) reputation for the lowest intellectual standards at the university. Is this the expression of Russia's traditional weakness in individualism, rationalism and legalism, or of legal nihilism due to the law's humble place in Marxian ideology? Whatever the combination, I met no young Russian excited by the law. Law as a precious achievement, a distillation of human intellect, reason and compassion, a protector of rights and dignity, 'due process', 'equal protection', 'the rule of law' – this side of it was missing. The generosity and creative genius of the Russian spirit flow in different channels.*

It is safe to say that the attitude here portrayed is by no means confined to Russia or to 'Eastern' countries. It is probably typical of men everywhere when they have developed no sense of participation, even vicariously, in their governments. And such men are to be found, in varying numbers and for varying reasons, in all countries.

The health and sickness of a legal system

There is no intention here to mediate among these various attitudes towards law. Under particular circumstances all of them can be justified or at least become inevitable. They have been set forth at length because they reflect the complexities and hidden antinomies that run through the fabric of the law.

The suggestion that the law contains 'complexities and hidden antinomies' may arouse some scepticism. It may be said that though reactions to the law – like those towards the weather – may be complex and subtle, there is nothing about the notion of law itself that suggests such qualities. Individual laws, to be sure, may be complicated and forbiddingly so, with their endless paragraphs, their 'aforesaids' and 'provided howevers'. But

* George Feifer, *Justice in Moscow*, Simon and Schuster, 1964, p. 343.

about the notion of law itself there is no mystery. Everyone knows what it is and why it exists.

For men to live together successfully they need rules that will keep peace among them, make them deal justly with one another, and enable them to collaborate effectively. Since men are likely to differ about what these rules should be, it is necessary to set up some procedure by which the rules may be authoritatively declared, for example, by enactment of a legislative assembly or by judgment of a court. Hopefully, in a democratic society the more important and pervasive legal rules will reflect a consensus, though, of course, many rules will relate to specialized activities on which there could be no informed opinion among the population as a whole. Since no role can be so phrased as to be absolutely certain in its application to all cases, it is essential to appoint judges with the power to make a binding interpretation of the rules and to determine authoritatively what their application should be in disputed cases. Finally, some incentive to obey the rules must be provided; we cannot leave the man who flouts the law in the same situation as one who faithfully accepts its restraints. Either the man who breaks the rules must suffer some disadvantage or the man who follows them must be given some reward. The latter arrangement is uncommon, but it is not unknown in the law. An example would be a tax rebate given to the owner of timber lands who follows certain officially prescribed cutting practices designed to guarantee a continuing supply of timber. More commonly, the method of the law is to impose some kind of unpleasantness on the rule-breaker, who may be fined or sentenced or have an award of damages assessed against him.

The account just given could obviously stand much qualification and expansion. But the gist of the matter would seem to be expressed by it. It contains no suggestion that there is anything subtle or complex about the notion of law or about establishing and administering a legal system.

This impression of simplicity, however, is an illusion. To perceive the full extent to which this is so we shall, in what follows, go behind the scenes and participate vicariously in the cares and concerns of those who are responsible for enacting, applying, and enforcing the law. This will be our preoccupation for a good many pages to come.

The plan of our attack is, then, the opposite of that which the reader might expect. He might anticipate that we would first give an account of the law itself as it appears in its different branches. Pursuing such a plan we might, for example, first take up the law of contracts and present a short account of its leading principles. We might then in similar fashion turn to the criminal law and so proceed through all the different sub-divisions of the law. We would then, against the background of a knowledge of legal rules thus imparted, take up some of the more subtle and difficult problems, such as those of interpreting ambiguous rules.

This order of presentation, however, would disserve the cause of understanding. There are pervasive problems that run through the whole legal system. One cannot understand its branches without having some insight into the nature of these problems. To try to learn the rules of contract law, for example, without this insight would be like trying to become a gardener by learning the names of flowers and plants without having any idea of the effects of sun and shade, heat and cold, compost and loam.

In attempting to convey an understanding of the problems faced by those who cultivate the garden of the law, we shall be especially concerned with situations where things go wrong, not radically and obviously wrong, but subtly and inconspicuously wrong. One cannot learn much about the problems of horticulture by viewing a garden laid flat by a hurricane or dried to straw by a drought. But one can often learn a great deal when one sees two plants of the same species growing in slightly different locations where one thrives and the other falters. So our primary concern here is not with gross failures of law – corruption, lawless despotisms, and tyrannical abuses of law – but with the small miscarriages that come through inattention and imperceptiveness and in spite of reasonably good intentions.

Another analogy – from medicine – may be helpful at this point. Aristotle long ago observed that we can learn what health is by considering situations in which it is missing. When we enjoy health it seems a thing too simple and transparent to offer any entry for analysis. 'Only in ill health does one realize the intricacy of the body . . .' So our interest here in diseases of the law is clinical, not morbid. We shall accordingly address ourselves chiefly to the subtler forms of legal pathology and not to missing limbs and organs.

In what follows, our interest will be chiefly directed towards the criminal law. There are several reasons for choosing this branch of the law for special attention in a discussion of the disorders to which legal systems are subject. Because the criminal law cuts so deeply into human life, any irregularities in its functioning must be of special concern. For the same reason its miscarriages are likely to be a subject of discussion and newspaper comment. Finally, for the lay observer the criminal law in some measure symbolizes the law as a whole. He understands generally what it is about and tends to take it as his model for legal processes generally. The selection of the most dramatic branch of the law in the ensuing discussion will, to be sure, introduce some distortions that will have to be corrected later when more prosaic and recondite branches of the law come under scrutiny. For the time being, however, its problems offer the most accessible entry to a perception of the problems of law generally.

The law in books and the law in action

We may begin by plunging headlong into a much-debated issue of legal philosophy. The issue, stated loosely, is this: Does the reality of law lie in words on paper or in human behaviour? In ecclesiastical terms, the choice is between the Word and the Deed. One does not have to be very precise about the meaning of this question to hazard a guess that the pragmatic temper of modern times will opt in favour of a view that sees the reality of law in human action and not in 'mere' words.

But let us examine the meaning of the question itself more closely. To do this we shall have to explore the kind of context out of which it can arise. Here, as elsewhere, we shall choose for our purposes the criminal law. In most countries today the law of crimes is statutory and there will ordinarily be a written Criminal Code defining what acts are criminal and what the appropriate punishments shall be. Where such a Code exists, it is normally understood that the courts are strictly bound by it, that is to say, they have no authority to create new crimes or to declare any act a violation of the law that is not included in the Code. *Nulla poena sine lege* – 'no punishment except in accordance with a [previous] law' – is a legal maxim generally respected in all civilized nations.

Suppose that a citizen wants to know whether some act he proposes to do is criminal. We are assuming that the question arises in an area of conduct where ordinary standards of moral behaviour are an insufficient guide. The citizen wants to know, for example, whether it is lawful for him to keep his news-stand open on the afternoon of a particular national holiday. He takes the question to an attorney. The attorney naturally turns in the first place to the Criminal Code. This is where the law 'is'. To be sure, the attorney may encounter some ambiguity in the relevant provisions and he may wish to consult the reports of judicial decisions to see how the courts have construed the Code. But if the courts have had occasion to interpret the Code, they do not by that fact consider that they have themselves created new law. On the contrary, they describe their role as that of drawing from the Code the proper rules for the decision of the cases before them. The 'law' remains – one is tempted to say, abides – in the Code.

Suppose it turns out that though the act the client proposes to do is plainly branded as criminal by the Code, for some time the provisions concerning it have fallen into disuse and prosecutors take no steps to enforce them. Here we seem to have a discrepancy between words and actions. By the words of the Code the act is criminal, but judged by the realities of official behaviour the act escapes any effective legal restraint. How shall we resolve this conflict? The answer that comes naturally to laymen and to practical lawyers – though not to all legal philosophers – is to say that of course the act remains a crime, but that the law making it criminal is simply not enforced. In the competition between words and actions to serve as the final test of law, here words, duly pronounced by legislative authority, seem obviously to win out.

The situation just discussed is one that can, and should, give rise to some disquietude. What about justice to the citizen who becomes the victim of an ambitious prosecutor who begins to enforce for the first time a statute that has been a dead letter for years? What of the possibility of favouritism in the enforcement of law? Later we shall return to these questions and consider the means open to a legal system to cure or prevent discrepancies between the law as it is written and the law as it is enforced. Meanwhile it is enough to note that such discrepancies can arise and that no simple and direct means for curing them exist.

Meanwhile let us take a quite different tack in approaching our main problem. Let us suppose that in a country called Erewhon there has existed for centuries a lawful, democratic, and constitutional government. In a time of crisis this government is overthrown by a dictator who expressly abrogates the old constitution and sets up a regime of his own. The leading officials of the overthrown government manage to escape to the territory of a friendly people where they establish a government in exile. The possible need for this measure has, in fact, been foreseen in the constitution under which they held office. It is there provided that in the event of an overthrow of the government, its officials should be authorized to transfer the seat of power to another nation. From that seat they are to exercise the powers conferred by their constitution, co-opting their successors as the original officials die or resign. The constitution provides that when the opportunity presents itself, this government may be transferred back to its original seat and that general elections should then be held in Erewhon six months after the return of the exiled government.

Now in such a situation it is plain that for some time the exiled government might be regarded as the true government of Erewhon. This view might reasonably be shared by most of the people of Erewhon, their exiled officials, and friendly nations. But as the years roll by, the hope for any return to power may gradually fade, and the time may come when it would be farcical to maintain that the 'true' governmental power resided in the exiled officials. A government that is all words on paper, that is permanently incapable of taking effective action, ceases to be a government. If it purports to enact legal rules governing happenings in Erewhon, these rules are no longer properly called laws because they bear no meaningful relation to the world of human affairs. In the contest between words and actions to serve as the test for law, in this case the test of effective action wins out.

Putting together the two situations we have discussed, we arrive at a conclusion that may be expressed metaphorically: When the tree of law is dead from the roots up, a legal system has ceased to exist. When only a twig is dead, we not only do not declare the whole tree dead (which is understandable), but we treat the twig itself as if it were still alive (which is puzzling).

We then face this paradox: At one end of the spectrum (we may call it the tree end), the existence of law is determined by the possibility of effective action; if this is precluded, then words on paper, once effective to determine the existence of law, lose this power. At the other end of the spectrum (the twig end), the existence of law is determined by enacted words, and not by the action those words stimulate.

The explanation for this shift in the test for law is really quite simple. We may express it by an analogy. When a vessel at sea begins to founder there comes a time when it must be given up as lost. But we do not give the order to abandon ship as soon as, let us say, a fuel pump begins to function erratically. So it is with the law. If the whole enterprise has failed, we abandon it. If only a small component part is performing badly, we work to keep the system going as best we can.

The analogy just suggested may seem inapt. After all, when a fuel pump falters we set about repairing it. When a holiday closing law is left unenforced we are content simply to say, 'Well, it no longer functions in the sense that it has any effect on human behaviour, but it is still law just the same.' This seems like trying to cure a badly functioning pump by the simple process of declaring it to be in order. But we must remember that the word 'law' never serves purely as a term descriptive of actual events; there inheres in it a sense of prescription, of what ought to be. If as soon as the prosecutor ceased to take active steps to secure compliance with a law, we declared the law no longer in force, we would be vesting in the prosecutor the power to repeal – by his indolence, prejudice, or corruption – a law duly enacted by the legislature. Obviously this is something that cannot be tolerated.

To the question with which we started – does the existence of law depend on words or on actions? – we have then so far given the answer: It is both. When we are concerned with the existence of a legal system as a whole, we find the test in action, that is, in its power to exert some measure of actual influence in human affairs. When our interest is in a particular legal rule that forms part of a legal system that continues to function as a going concern, we find the test in enacted words.

Reconciling the word and the deed

This double-headed solution of our problem plainly leaves certain difficulties unresolved. One has already been mentioned: the practical task of discovering ways of removing or alleviating the injustice that comes from sporadic and arbitrary law enforcement. The other is of a more theoretical nature. It raises the question whether there is any way of mediating between the opposing answers given to what seems essentially the same question, answering it one way in one context, another way in a different context. It is all very well to say that at one end of the spectrum the word 'law' describes the factual existence of a system of rules that are generally effective in human affairs, whereas at the other end it points to a specific legislative intention that does and must retain the force of law even though for the time being it is ineffectual. But what of the middle ground? How do we locate the crossover point where these opposed meanings make contact? Is there no general theory that will reduce the meaning of law to a single formulation, something like a words-action synthesis?

During the past half century many legal writers have addressed themselves to this question and have convinced themselves that it can be solved. The favoured solution runs in general along these lines: The reality of law is to be found in the decisions of courts, that is, in the actions they take concerning the controversies that are submitted to them for resolution. Let us state as persuasively as possible the arguments that can be made for this view.

Though much of the law today is statutory, this law is not actually applied to human affairs by the legislature which enacts it. That is the task of the courts. It is in the courtroom, then, that life and law intersect. Here it is that the Word becomes the Deed and in the process acquires a meaning that is identical with its projection into human affairs.

The most obvious objection to this view is that the courts in projecting the law into human relations may fail to carry out faithfully the meaning of the words enacted by the legislatures. Courts are not infallible; through mistake, sloth, or prejudice they may give the law a meaning in action quite different from that properly to be found in its words. When this occurs, the gap separating the Word from the Deed is reopened.

To this objection the answer has been made that the power of the court to interpret statutes is, in effect, an unlimited power to remake them. John Chipman Gray in his *The Nature and Sources of the Law* (1921) repeats a number of times a quotation from Bishop Hoadly: 'Whoever hath an *absolute authority* to *interpret* any written or spoken laws, it is *he* who is truly the *Law-giver* to all intents and purposes, and not the person who first wrote or spoke them.' Even so conservative and untheoretic a lawyer as Charles Evans Hughes (Associate Justice of the Supreme Court of the United States, 1910–16; Chief Justice, 1930–41) once declared, 'We are under a Constitution, but the Constitution is what the judges say it is ...' The notion back of these quotations is essentially the same as that of the familiar saying, 'The king can do no wrong.' In an absolute monarchy this means not that the king cannot act mistakenly or immorally, but that he cannot act illegally since it is he who makes the law.

If we grant to the courts an unlimited power to give meaning to the words of the law at the point where these words are converted into action, the problem of removing the gap between law as human behaviour and law as words on paper seems to be solved. The Word and the Deed have become one. So we find Gray insisting that a proper definition of law conceives of it as the rules applied by the courts in the decision of litigated controversies, and that this definition holds whether the rules were originally court-made or were legislatively enacted. The most famous expression of this point of view is Holmes's 'predictive theory of law': 'The prophecies of what the courts will do in fact, and nothing more pretentious, are what I mean by the law.'

At this point everything seems in order until we recall that we still have made no progress in solving the problem with which we began – the case of a criminal statute, clear in meaning so there is little difficulty in predicting how the courts would apply it, but left completely unenforced by the prosecuting authorities. What we have here is a lack of jibe between words and actions at a level below that of the courts. In this arena it is impossible to maintain that the courtroom is the place where words and actions inevitably meet and are mediated because infractions of the law are not brought to court at all.

At one time some writers flirted with the notion of defining law as the behaviour of courts *and other public officials.* Such a definition would satisfy the pragmatic yearning to see reality in what happens, not in what words say should happen. But this would be nonsense. There is a sense in which a court cannot misapply the law; having the final say in its interpretation, what the court says makes the law. Although we may criticize the interpretation a court puts on a statute, that interpretation, after all, determines our rights and duties. But no one in his right senses would apply the same principle to the behaviour of a policeman or prosecutor.

Keeping judicial action in line with legislative intent

At this point let us abandon, for the time being, further effort towards some comprehensive reconciliation of the view that sees the reality of law in human action and that which considers it as a prescription of what ought to occur rather than a description of what does in fact occur. Let us turn instead to the practical measures open to a society to prevent the law from meaning one thing in books and something quite different in practice. When we have viewed more closely the problems actually confronted in creating and managing a legal system, we shall be in a better position to see what law 'is', just as we can see more clearly what horticulture 'is' when we have some notion of the problems that must be faced in trying to make plants grow properly.

First, what can we do about cases where courts misconstrue or misapply statutes enacted by the legislature? No one can truly understand this problem without a realization of the difficulties that attend the problem of construing statutes. We shall have repeated occasion to deal explicitly with those difficulties. For the time being it will be enough to put down one source of obfuscation. This is the notion current among laymen that lawyers, with all their forbidding jargon, have some uncanny ability to convey meaning to one another with great exactitude. Outside the area of a few terms of art, there is nothing to this belief. To fill in the spaces between their 'whereases' and 'provided howevers' lawyers have no resources except those available to any user of language. Most lawyers through experience in draftsmanship gain a considerable ability to anticipate the less obvious cases that may arise under a statute. The enactment drafted by an experienced lawyer is thus less likely to be plagued by the problem of the unforeseen case than is one drafted by a layman. But in expressing the core of meaning that constitutes the essence of a statute the lawyer has no special resources at his command. In projecting his intention into the future he must, like the layman, launch on the shifting currents of life a fragile vessel of words built from the materials that are available to everyone.

How sadly lacking is any general understanding of what it means to 'interpret and apply the law' was revealed in a statement made in a political campaign. A candidate for the presidency of the United States, when asked what his policy would be with reference to judicial appointments, replied that he would 'see that the federal judges are of the highest quality. If they don't follow the law there is always removal for cause.'* The casual manner in which it is here proposed that judges who do not 'follow the law' be removed from office obviously ignores the ancient problem: Who shall guard the guardians? In this case: Who shall judge whether the judges are judging by the law?

In all civilized countries the independence of the judiciary is regarded as one of the most important ingredients of civic health. To impeach a judge for misconduct in office is viewed as a drastic remedy to be applied only in extreme cases and under procedures designed to guarantee the strictest impartiality.

Furthermore, removing a judge from the bench and passing his decision in review cannot in the nature of things undo the harm caused by judicial misconduct. Men have to rely on the decisions of courts and shape their affairs by them. They enter into the very structure of society itself. If a judge has been guilty of misconduct and if, after his removal from office, we try to prick out the errors he has woven into the fabric of the law, we shall soon discover that our task has no natural stopping place. We may end by unravelling completely the fabric we intended to mend.

How untidy and perplexing a task it is to undo the consequences of judicial misconduct came clearly into view in an incident that arose during the 1930s in the Second Federal Circuit. There was here involved the most unusual case of a judge who was found guilty of accepting bribes from litigants to decide cases in their favour. What, then, should be done with the cases in which he had taken bribes? It was decided that first they should all be reheard by a reconstituted court.†

* Associated Press, *Boston Herald*, 20 July 1964, p. 7.
† One might suggest at this point, why not reverse them all without a

In the actual cases in question certain of the tainted decisions involved the validity of patents and therefore touched on a very technical and somewhat indefinite branch of the law. In a number of the cases the convicted judge had written opinions supporting a judgment that patents in question were invalid. A period of years ensued before any doubt of these decisions arose. Affected parties had meanwhile adjusted their relations to the assumption that the patents had no legal force. When the cases were reheard certain of them were reversed so that the patents in question were finally held to be valid. In one of these cases, involving a patented cigarette lighter, a period of some seven years elapsed between the time when the patent was held to be invalid and the final reversal of the tainted judgment. What then should be done with the lost years during which the patent holder was deprived of profits and royalties he would have enjoyed had the first decision properly held his patent to be valid? The only solution found for this problem was to secure the passage of a special act of Congress extending the life of the patent by a period equal to that during which it was assumed to be invalid. This, at best, produced a rough justice, 'rough' because seven years in the 1940s cannot be the same as seven years in the 1930s, especially when account is taken of the effects of technological progress that would tend to reduce the value of the patents. But this was not the end. Parties who were not litigants in the law suits that produced the tainted decisions had to some indefinite degree relied on the

---

rehearing? Losing his case is not too harsh a penalty for the litigant who bribes a judge. A little reflection will demonstrate that this easy way out is barred. That a judge has taken a bribe does not necessarily mean that his decision was incorrect. As a matter of fact the judge in question was a member of a three-man court, so that at least one of his colleagues, innocent of any wrongdoing, had in each of the tainted cases to agree with the decision actually rendered. To reverse these decisions without regard to their merits would be to visit an injustice on innocent parties who, though not parties to the litigation that produced them, may have relied on the decisions as statements of the law and guided their conduct by them. Furthermore, even those directly affected by the decisions may have been innocent of any complicity in the bribe, as would be the case where the overzealous officer of a corporation paid a bribe without the knowledge of his stockholders.

legal implications of those decisions in judging the validity of related patents. Finally, one of the decisions had become a leading case in patent law and had been cited and relied on by other courts in deciding the validity of still other patents.*

The considerations just passed in review show how vital is the principle of the independence of the judiciary. This principle is recognized as a fundamental of civilized government everywhere. It is usually rested on the notion that the judge cannot act fairly and justly if he is subject to outside pressures. Our discussion shows that there is another dimension to the problem. This lies in the heavy cost incurred when an attempt is made, after the event, to correct the consequences of a judge's yielding to outside pressures. The case we discussed involved, of course, the most outrageous departure from judicial proprieties, the selling of a decision for a fee. One can imagine how all the difficulties attending that case would be magnified if it became the common practice to remove a judge for 'not following the law', retrospectively attempting to reassemble the broken pieces left behind by his misconduct or his lack of perception. For good or ill, the necessities of government demand that we choose for the bench only men of the highest integrity and intelligence and that once placed in office they be accorded a wide sphere of independence from every kind of outside influence.

Suppose, however, that a judge does make an outrageous interpretation of a statute. Is there no remedy here? History offers one such remedy that has a certain specious logic about it. If there is doubt about the interpretation of a statute, or the judge mistakes its meaning, why not let the correction be made directly by the agency that issued the statute, namely, the legislature? If I am working in a business establishment and I receive an order from a superior that I can't quite make out, I ask him what he meant. Why not follow this sensible procedure where laws are concerned?

Over the centuries there have in fact been advocates of this solution and it has from time to time been adopted. The pro-

* See J. Borkin, *The Corrupt Judge*, Clarkson N. Potter, Inc., New York, 1962, pp. 23–93, esp. 53–9.

cedure of referring the doubtful statute to its author has acquired a name in the literature of jurisprudence. It is called 'authentic interpretation'. The Code of Justinian provided:

... if anything shall seem doubtful, let it be referred by the judges to the Imperial Throne and it shall be made plain by Imperial authority, to which alone is given the right both to establish and to interpret laws. (I, 17, 2, 21.)

This device has been tried in more recent times in certain European countries, the legislature standing of course in the place of the Imperial Throne. But this procedure has always failed, and no thoughtful adviser would recommend it to any government today.

What are the reasons for this failure? These reasons will be examined here with care and with a greater thoroughness than would be appropriate if our only object were to demonstrate the unwisdom of the proposed solution. Our concern is not merely with this immediate problem but also, and more especially, with the task of conveying to the reader a general insight into the special nature of the problems that arise in creating and administering a legal system. The problem before us happens to be especially useful in conveying that insight and it will accordingly be exploited for that purpose. In later discussions we can then build on the understanding that has been achieved here.

The first question anyone experienced in dealing with legal problems would ask is one that would not be likely to occur to most laymen at all. It is a question of procedure. Men who participate in affairs – whether in politics, law, business, or education – characteristically become, as their experience accumulates, increasingly concerned with *how* things should be done and not just with *what* should be done. One can cite eminent men, including Senator Paul H. Douglas and Wilhelm von Humboldt, who have described a deepening concern for procedure as the principal change they underwent between youth and mature age.

What procedural problems would be involved if the legislature were given the opportunity to overrule mistaken judicial interpretations of its statutes? There are many. But one that would have to be faced at the outset is: By what method would the cases decided by courts be brought up for review by the legislature? Without considering mixed forms, there are three possible procedures. One would be to have the legislature itself watch over the decisions as they came out and order up for review any that seemed doubtful. Obviously any such procedure would impose an impossible burden on the legislature or its committees. No such comprehensive review of the work of lower courts has ever been undertaken by any appellate tribunal. To be compelled to work under any such pervasive scrutiny would destroy the independence of the judge and rob his office of any personal sense of satisfaction. He would become like an anxious pupil trying to do his sums with teacher constantly looking over his shoulder.

A second procedure would be to leave it to the judge himself to decide whether a case be referred to the legislature. This has in fact been the procedure generally followed in those historical instances where the judicial interpretation of statutes has in practice been subjected to legislative review. The procedure has the peculiarity that, starting with a distrust of the judge's ability to perceive the statute's meaning, it ends by allowing him to pass on his own qualifications for that task. The bold judge can protect himself from legislative interference by the simple device of refusing to admit doubts. The timid judge, on the other hand, has open to him a way of shirking his responsibilities by declaring every case to be doubtful.

There remains the procedure of allowing the litigant defeated in court to take the initiative himself in appealing his case to the legislature. The foreseeable consequence would be that the legislature would designate a special committee to hear such appeals. If the volume of appeals became appreciable, the members of this committee would have to withdraw in large measure from the ordinary work of legislation and would become to all intents and purposes a court. Thus a procedure designed to let the legislature say what it meant by its own language would end by adding just another bench of judges at the end of the chain of appeal. This development can, indeed, be traced historically. Viewed in the light of history, the distinction between judicial and legislative functions, today taken for granted, is a comparatively modern development. American state legislatures in the early days decreed divorces, granted discharges in bankruptcy, and rendered a wide variety of decisions that we consider today to be reserved to the judiciary. The British House of Lords, composed of what are called the Law Lords, is today not a legislative body, but a court, being quite distinct from the House of Lords as a deliberative assembly. This separation of functions has come about gradually, the House of Lords originally having exercised its judicial and legislative powers as one body.

Let us put to one side the question of the procedure to be followed in bringing the case for review before the legislature, and address ourselves now to the question whether it is wise to accord to the legislature any special competence in construing its own language.

Suppose the legislature passes a statute which makes it a misdemeanour 'to sleep in any railway station'. Two cases are brought to court. One involves an alcoholic derelict who came to the station dragging a tattered blanket, spread himself out for the night, and was then arrested while his eyes were still open. In the other case a neat and orderly traveller, waiting at midnight for a train that was five hours overdue, had just fallen asleep sitting upright when he was arrested. Has either of these men violated the statute, and if so, which? Is it likely that the legislature would have any way of answering this question that would not be available to a court? (If the case seems easy on the principle that *sleep* means sleep and not lying down in order to go to sleep, consider the following problem: A sightseeing tourist visits a colonial mansion that has a sign reading: 'Washington slept here.' When he returns home the tourist consults his history books and discovers that, although Washington did indeed go to bed in the house in question, he lay awake all night trying to work out some plan to defeat the Redcoats. Is the tourist entitled to a return of the admission fee on the ground that he was induced to pay it by a false statement?)

The plain fact is that in most cases where doubt can arise

as to whether a particular situation is covered by a statute, no intellectual resources are available to the legislature in deciding the questions that are not equally available to the judge, who normally has, furthermore, the advantage of more experience in dealing with such questions. Let us suppose, however, a case where the legislature, or at least certain of its members, can fairly be said to have a special knowledge of what was meant. A statute, for example, makes it unlawful to 'carry concealed on the person any pistol, revolver, firearm, or other like weapon'. The defendant is arrested for carrying a slingshot in his pocket. He is tried by a court which finds that he did not violate the statute; 'other like weapon' in the context of the statute means some device for propelling a bullet by an explosion. The case is referred to the legislature. It appears that when the statute was under discussion the question of slingshots was raised and the draftsman explained orally to a considerable number of the legislators that slingshots were covered by the words 'or other like weapon'. It is perfectly plain that when a man is accused of a crime, his guilt ought to depend on how he might reasonably interpret, or at least how his lawyer might reasonably interpret, the statute defining the crime in question. The issue ought to be not what the legislature meant to say, but what it succeeded in saying. It is evident that this is a question that can be tried more objectively by a court than by those who had a hand in drafting the statute.

There is indeed on this matter a statement that has become classic. When the interpretation of an English statute was once in debate Lord Nottingham is reported to have said, 'I had some reason to know the meaning of this law; for it had its first rise from me.' In Campbell's *Lives of the Lord Chancellors of England*, this comment is made, 'If Lord Nottingham drew it, he was the less qualified to construe it; the author of an act considering more what he privately intended than the meaning he has expressed.'*

* Vol. 3, 3rd ed., 1848, p. 423.

*Preserving the integrity of the law
at the point of enforcement*

In the discussion just concluded we were concerned to inquire
what measures can be taken to keep the judicial interpretation
of statutes in jibe with the intention expressed in those statutes
– by what means, in other words, we can make sure that judges
'follow the law'. Our modest conclusion was that all that can
be done safely and effectively is to choose able and honest men
as judges and to invest their office with a degree of independence that will make them secure against outside influences.

It is now time to return to a lower and broader level of the
legal pyramid, that entrusted to the agencies of law enforcement, chiefly the police and prosecuting attorneys. The law
cannot enforce itself. Some human agency must be charged
with that responsibility; some official of government has to
initiate the proceedings by which the law will be applied. If
the discharge of the responsibility is lax, tainted with favouritism, or perverted by corruption, then the law is, in effect,
modified and rewritten in the process of being applied.

To reduce the risk of this distortion, one remedy that might
recommend itself would be to subject the work of the police
and of prosecuting attorneys to the supervision of the courts.
The courts, after all, have an opportunity to observe the daily
functioning of the agencies of enforcement; if matters are not
in order at the level of the legal system, they will be in the best
position to know what has gone wrong and what remedy will
most effectively put things straight. Furthermore, the same
qualities of detachment and of impartiality that qualify a man
for judicial office are equally desirable in this supervisory role.

The assignment of any such function to the judiciary, however, would involve a most dangerous confusion of roles. The
notion that the roles of prosecutor and judge should be held
by different persons, standing towards one another in some
aloofness, is so commonplace to us that we easily forget how
painfully it was arrived at and how fragile it remains even
today. It should be remembered that the prosecutor performs
a function of considerable complexity. The proper discharge

of his office requires many exercises of judgement. He must often, for example, decide how far to pursue a complaint that on its face seems unfounded, balancing a likely waste of scarce time and energy against the remote possibility that the complaint may turn out to be justified. Any judicial involvement in questions of this delicacy would inevitably compromise the court's position as a forum for the final and impartial determination of disputed issues.

We should remember that in the 'inquisitorial court' the roles of prosecutor, defender, and judge are combined in one person or group of persons. It is no accident that such a court commonly holds its sessions in secret. The usual explanation for this is that the methods by which it extracts confessions cannot stand public scrutiny. But the reason runs deeper. The methods employed by an inquisitorial court, even if open to the public, could scarcely be a subject of meaningful observation by an outsider. It is only when the roles of prosecutor, defender, and judge are separated that a process of decision can take on an order and coherence that will make it understandable to an outside audience and convince that audience that all sides of the controversy have been considered. A separation of the roles involved in a judicial decision is therefore an essential for anything that can be called a sound *public* order of law. It has, in fact, been suggested that resort to torture and techniques of brainwashing comes primarily from a desire of the inquisitorial court to obtain formal confessions that will convince the world of the rightness of its decisions, something that could not be done through its essentially formless methods of inquiry even if they were open to public scrutiny.

It may be said that these remarks are rather beside the point for modern constitutional democracies. It may be thought that in such societies there is little danger of a return to 'Star Chamber' methods. But to find reassurance in such reflections is to ignore the subtleties of the problem and to forget that a full separation of functions is not achieved simply by formally assigning different roles to different persons.

It is, for example, a commonplace among those familiar with

the daily operation of legal systems that judges on the lowest level of the criminal law have a strong tendency to identify themselves with the police force. In a moment of candour a judge holding such a position is likely to confess that where there is a conflict of testimony between the arresting police-man and the accused he will almost automatically accept as true the statement made by the officer. The reason for this preference is that the judge sincerely believes any other course 'would impair the morale of the police', who occupy a difficult, dangerous, and insufficiently appreciated role in our society. Any pangs of conscience stirred by this largely automatic preference may be quieted by the reflection that in most cases the incidents preceding an arrest are confused and obscure, so that memories of them on both sides are apt to be uncertain and heavily coloured by self-interest. A surrender to this line of rationalization leads easily to a confusion of the roles of judge and prosecutor in which is lost the separation of functions essential to a civilized system of justice.

It is often convenient to think of a legal system as forming a kind of hierarchy of authority; we have ourselves spoken of 'the legal pyramid'. The apparatus of the criminal law may be fitted into this picture. At the top is the legislature declaring what acts shall be crimes and what the appropriate punish-ments shall be. On the second tier we have the courts resolving disputed issues of fact and determining the proper application of statutory language to individual cases. On the third level we have the agencies of enforcement detecting crime, receiving complaints, and bringing before the courts charges that indi-viduals have committed criminal acts.

Though this pyramidal conception has some value, it must not be taken to imply anything like a military chain of command or even an analogy to the vertical organization of a business firm. In the law each level of the hierarchy has its distinctive role to discharge. Any direct encroachment on other roles, either upward or downward, can destroy the integrity of the whole legal process.

These remarks should not, of course, be taken to imply that the prosecutor's office should never be subject to outside investigation, and still less that any such immunity should be enjoyed by the practices of the police. What is meant is that any such investigation should be initiated by some specially constituted body functioning outside the normal framework of law enforcement.

This leaves the question whether there are any impersonal or institutional measures available that may serve as a kind of prophylaxis against the introduction of distortions into the law at the level of enforcement. One such measure, of quite limited utility, lies in the doctrine of *the desuetude of statutes*, according to which a statute left long enough unenforced will no longer be regarded by the courts as having any legal effect. An American judge once vividly described the evil against which this doctrine is directed when he observed that 'an ancient sleeping statue' may 'do great mischief, if suddenly brought into action'.

It is an open question whether the 'mischief' which the doctrine of desuetude is designed to remove may not be equalled by the 'mischief' introduced by the doctrine itself. The main objection to it is the uncertainty it entails. The period of disuse necessary to nullify a statute may become inactive for a long time simply because it is not being violated; a return of the evil it sought to prevent may make it quite appropriate to loosen up its rusty hinges and put it in action again. In another situation a rapid change in circumstances may within a relatively short time make a statute seem like an anachronism. In any event the doctrine of desuetude has had in all legal systems a very limited and cautious application.* For the anachronistic statute a better remedy may be found through reinterpretation in the light of new conditions; as Gray remarks with some irony, 'It is not as speedy or as simple a process to interpret a statute out of existence as to repeal it, but with time and patient skill it can often be done.'†

The institution of the *investigating magistrate* is another measure for preserving the integrity of the law at the level of en-

---

* See John Chipman Gray, *The Nature and Sources of the Law*, 2nd ed., The Macmillan Co., New York, 1921, pp. 189–97, pp. 329–34.

† ibid., p. 192.

forcement. In this case the measure is directed not towards curing the evils of a lax or sporadic enforcement, but towards the evils of an opposite nature, those resulting from an excess of zeal on the part of the prosecutor. Under the system in question, before a criminal charge may be brought before the regular courts it must be investigated by a special official and, in effect, certified as deserving trial in court. The investigating magistrate is thus a kind of quasi-judge standing halfway between the prosecutor and the regular court. The danger of the institution lies precisely in this twilight zone of function which it occupies. The certification of a case for trial inevitably tends to confirm the criminal charge against the suspect, thus creating what may amount in practice to a strong presumption of guilt. The element of prejudgment involved constitutes a threat to the integrity of the trial in open court; the accused has, in effect, had a kind of half-trial in advance of the real trial, and this half-trial is conducted, not *before* but *by* a kind of half-judge who acts essentially as an inquisitorial court. In those countries where it is a part of the legal system, the role of the investigating magistrate continues to be a subject of some debate, and even where it is generally accepted, there is always some lingering concern lest it become the subject of inconspicuous abuse.

The institution of the investigating magistrate is a part of the tradition of the countries following 'the civil law', that is, those countries whose legal systems derive historically from the Roman model. The investigating magistrate is unknown, at least under that designation, in the countries deriving their legal systems from the English model. In these countries the institution bearing the closest resemblance to the investigating magistrate is the grand jury. In the course of its long history the grand jury has in fact been accused of permitting abuses similar to those sometimes charged against the investigating magistrate. The fact that the presentment (accusation) of the grand jury has to be brought in by the verdict of a panel of jurors offers an obvious safeguard against the possibility of a bureaucratic abuse of office, though in times of public excitement the participation of a dozen or two 'good men and true' may merely serve to lend a veneer of due process to expressions of mass hysteria. At any rate the grand jury – despite the attention focused on it when it is in session – forms a very minor part of the system of criminal law taken as a whole, and there are those who consider that even that minor role ought to be eliminated.

Curbing irresponsibility in the making of laws

During most of the world's history the preoccupations of legal philosophy have been with the substance of the law and with the task of assigning a proper role to each of the various offices and institutions that make up a legal system. Since the legal system itself was conceived as a collaborative enterprise involving different and complementary roles, it was believed that any one of its components might display a failure of function.

In more recent times legal philosophy has inclined increasingly to concentrate on the hierarchic structure of law; the task it has set itself has tended to be that of defining precisely each of the elements in a vertical chain of command. This preoccupation leads easily to the view that the supreme law-giving authority cannot itself impair the integrity of the law. On the lower reaches of the hierarchy men act irresponsibly toward the law when they fail to carry out faithfully the commands of their superior. But the supreme lawgiver cannot himself be out of step since it is he who calls the tune.

In reality, some of the most grievous offences against the integrity of the law come not from the lower levels of the hierarchy of offices, but from the legislator himself. The catalogue of his sins is a long one. It includes vague and contradictory laws, laws changed capriciously and in response to passing political pressures, esoteric legal compulsions hidden in obscure corners of the code book, and a hundred and one other ways of writing confusion into what is supposed to be the prime source of social order.

There is not space here to consider all of the ways in which the lawgiver may act irresponsibly towards the law. We shall consider only a few examples of legislative misbehaviour that have a contemporary interest.

One of the most serious of these offences is that of passing (or retaining on the statute books) laws that are not intended to be enforced at all. Such laws offer to the legislator an easy way of dodging difficult political issues. He may vote for a particular law in order to appease one faction, and at the same time count on the prosecutor not to enforce the law, thus insuring that the opposing faction will not be offended. A prime example of this abuse is to be found in laws against the sale of contraceptive devices. Most such laws are left completely without enforcement and are openly violated; those who favour retaining them on the books would not uncommonly be the last to insist on their effective enforcement.

Laws prohibiting the sale of alcoholic beverages furnish another example of laws that are likely to be enforced imperfectly or not enforced at all. The failure of such laws is usually thought to demonstrate that the lawgiver cannot impose on frail human nature demands that go beyond what is required by ordinary notions of right and wrong. Yet in fact it is often the same citizen who originally supports the passage of such laws who later connives at their violation. These laws jibe well enough with his notions of right and wrong; the trouble is they do not jibe with his capacity to act on his own professed convictions. Such irresolutions can be forgiven in an amorphous public opinion faced with no special responsibilities; it is less easy to forgive the legislator's complicity in writing them into law. The failure of prohibition does not so much illustrate a lawgiver out of touch with public opinion, as one too closely in touch with it and unable, or unwilling, to rise above its confusions in the making of laws.

Another common sin of the legislator consists in passing laws that are intended to be enforced only in selected cases. The chief of police of a New England town once declared to the press that he believed in a strict curfew law, 'selectively enforced'. 'Selective enforcement' in this case means that the policeman decides for himself who ought to be sent home from the street; legislative candour would suggest that if this is the intention it ought to be expressd in the law itself, instead of being concealed behind words that are 'strict' and categorical.

The popularity of strictly phrased laws designed for selective enforcement derives from a variety of motives. Some are by no means sinister, but none is worthy of a conscientious lawgiver. In the case of the curfew law, perhaps nothing more discreditable is involved than an unwillingness to acknowledge in the words of the statute itself the element of discretion that must be exercised in effectuating its purposes. Sometimes the determinative factor lies in the difficulty of drafting a statute that will satisfactorily discriminate between harmless and pernicious forms of the same activity. The difficulty becomes particularly acute in drafting statutes designed to outlaw commercialized gambling. It is no easy matter to draft such a statute so as to exclude the friendly game of penny ante, the charity raffle, and the church-sponsored bingo party, especially since commercialized gambling can sometimes be given the appearance of serving worthy causes. The easy escape from these problems of finding language that will make the necessary distinctions is to enact a broadly phrased statute, admitting no exceptions, and then count on the prosecutor to use 'discretion' in enforcing it. In judging the dangers of this practice we should recall that if the prosecutor becomes sufficiently accustomed to such statutes, it will be hard to wean him away from them. For they greatly facilitate his labours. When he takes a defendant to court under a 'strict' statute he has assurance in advance that he will not lose his case because of quibbles over the precise scope of exceptions written into the law. Furthermore, his relations with the accused are enhanced; to protestations that what was done was really innocent, he can say, 'It's not my idea. Just read the statute and see for yourself what it says.' Out of the 'understanding' thus induced, it may not be difficult to obtain a confession of guilt with a recommendation of leniency.

A companion piece to the law destined for selective enforcement is the law imposing preposterously severe penalties for minor offences. The ordinary citizen, thumbing his way through the statute book, may be startled to come upon some minor infraction burdened with a fine running into thousands of dollars and threatening the offender with economic ruin by a cancellation of his licence to carry on some business or profession. The uninitiated is likely to ask, 'Is this act really so wicked that it has to carry so drastic a punishment?' The answer is usually that the threatened penalties are not really intended to be applied at all, but rather to be used by the prosecutor as a club with which to obtain a confession from the accused and perhaps his collaboration in the pursuit of other offenders.

There is one broad branch of the criminal law where the integrity of law enforcement seems threatened by a natural tendency toward deterioration. This is the law concerned with what have been called 'crimes without victims' – such offences as prostitution, traffic in narcotics, and homosexual acts between consenting adults. Crimes of this nature require a willing participant and, regardless of whether his own act constitutes a crime, he is generally the last person likely to bring a complaint to the police. This whole 'borderland of the criminal law' is, for quite understandable reasons, no favourite of police and prosecutors. The difficulty of detecting offences tends almost inevitably towards a selective and sporadic enforcement. Curiously, though many charged with the enforcement of such laws believe that some of them, at least, ought not to be on the books at all, those sharing this view will often work to secure legislation that will stiffen the penalties attached to their violation. The reason for this paradoxical stand has already been suggested. Where the enforcement of a law is especially difficult, the police and prosecutors are likely to welcome the weapon which a threat of drastic punishment confers on them; with its help they are in a position to induce confessions and recruit informers.

Surely if the law has its seamy side it is to be found in the areas just suggested, where the methods of its enforcement may become almost as sordid as the activities that they are intended to suppress. But why is it that laws of this sort are enforced by such questionable methods, if, indeed, they are enforced at all? To answer this question we must recall that no one works well on a task that has no clearly defined purpose. One of the principal aims of the criminal law is to deter men from criminal acts, and when the agencies of enforcement believe that they are advancing this cause their task takes on meaning and direction. It is unlikely, however, that the drug addict will undergo the tortures of withdrawal simply to save himself a stretch in jail or that the homosexual will surrender his peculiar gratifications because they have been declared illegal. We should also recall in this connection that the offences in question are 'crimes without victims'. When a man's house has been robbed or his brother murdered, he is likely to take his complaint vigorously to the police and demand action. His presence on the scene dramatizes the need for law enforcement and gives sense and purpose to the work of the police and district attorney. In contrast, the absence of a prosecuting witness surrounds 'crimes without victims' with an entirely different atmosphere. Here it is the police who must assume the initiative. If they attempt to work without the aid of informers, they must resort to spying, and this spying is rendered all the more distasteful because what is spied upon is sordid and pitiable.

The whole area of 'crimes without victims' requires sober re-examination. Here an ounce of dispassionate sociological study is worth a ton of moral indignation, whether that indignation be directed toward the police or towards the unfortunate creatures they must pursue.

Removing obscurities as to what the law is trying to do – the purpose of the criminal law

One who has followed up to this point the account here given of 'pervasive problems of the law' may be inclined to say of these problems something like this: The ills and disorders of a legal system – at least those that come about despite reasonably good intention – can all be attributed to the fact that those concerned with the law are not clear as to what it is they are trying to do. If the law as a whole could be assigned some understandable general purpose, and if each separate law carried its own distinct purpose, plainly stated, then all these difficulties would disappear. Judges would then know how to interpret the law, the agencies of enforcement would know what their task was, and the general public would understand what was going on and would be able to pass an intelligent judgment on it. Finally, if the legislator were compelled to clarify his aims and to set them forth plainly, he would not be able to visit his obfuscations on the work of others. Everyone's task would then receive new meaning and direction. In other words, what we need, it may be said, is a good dose of the simple wisdom Hobbes expressed when he wrote:

... in all your actions, look often upon what you would have, as the thing that directs all your thoughts in the way to attain it. (*Leviathan,* part I, ch. 3.)

The need for this simple cure may seem peculiarly acute in the branch of the law with which we have so far been chiefly concerned, the criminal law. This branch of the law is notoriously afflicted by disputes as to what it is for. There are commonly said to be four 'theories' of the criminal law, that is, four distinct notions about what it should be trying to do. Let us at this point allow the famous mathematician, Norbert Wiener, the father of cybernetics, to state what these theories are and to express some of his distress that the law of crimes cannot make up its mind among discrepant ideas about what it is for:

Where the law of Western countries is at present least satisfactory is on the criminal side. Law seems to consider punishment, now as a threat to discourage other possible criminals, now as a ritual act of expiation on the part of the guilty man, now as a device for removing him from society and for protecting the latter from the danger of repeated misconduct, and now as an agency for the social and the moral reform of the individual. These are four different tasks, to be accomplished by four different methods; and unless we know an accurate way of proportioning them, our whole attitude to the criminal will be at cross-purposes. At present, the criminal law speaks now in one language, and now in another. Until we in the community have made up our minds that what we really want is expiation, or removal, or reform, or the discouragement of potential criminals, we shall get none of these, but only a confusion in which crime breeds more crime. Any code which is made, one fourth on the eighteenth-century British prejudice in favor of hanging, one fourth on the removal of the criminal from society, one fourth on a halfhearted policy of reform, and one fourth on the policy of hanging up a dead cow to scare away the rest, is going to get us precisely nowhere.

Let us put it this way: the first duty of the law, whatever the second and third ones are, is to know what it wants.*

These are strong words. Let us take them seriously and see what can be done to carry out the programme they propose.

First, it may be said – and it *has* been said many times – that we should start by purging the law entirely of the notion that its function is to make the guilty man 'pay' for his crime. This justification for the criminal law has been castigated as brutal and primitive, as an anachronistic survival, in Wiener's words, of 'the eighteenth-century British prejudice in favor of hanging'. It should be eliminated entirely, so it is said, from a civilized system of justice.

But the first question that must be faced is, *Can* it be eliminated? If there were no punishment of criminals it is reasonable to suppose that many acts now penalized by the state would become objects of private revenge. An unregulated private vengeance would inevitably degenerate into a war of reprisals and counter-reprisals. Such a condition is by no means unknown in primitive societies. One of the ancient roots of the modern criminal law can be discerned when social control was first asserted over acts of private vengeance and they were made subject to a kind of tariff of permitted, but limited, retributions.

There is a famous remark by Sir James Fitzjames Stephen to the effect that the criminal law bears to the instinct of revenge the same relation that the institution of marriage bears to the sexual instinct. Both regularize and control a deep impulse of human nature that if not given legitimate expression is bound to find disruptive outlets. Now it is apparent that this explanation or justification for punishment cannot be extended

* Norbert Wiener, *The Human Use of Human Beings*, Houghton Mifflin Co., Boston, 1950, pp. 116–17.

to the whole spectrum of crimes as they appear in a modern criminal code. It presupposes some person deeply injured by a crime committed against himself or someone close to him. It has no application to what have been called 'crimes without victims'. It has only an attenuated relevance to crimes where the 'victim' is the public interest, as, for example, where the criminal act consists in an embezzlement of public funds. While such an act may arouse a general indignation, it seems unlikely that even the most public-spirited citizen would feel any impulse to work physical violence on the embezzler.

At this point, however, there enters another possible justification for the penal or retributive theory of criminal law. It will be recalled that, in one of his descriptions of this theory, Wiener spoke of it as calling for 'a ritual act of expiation on the part of the guilty man'. Now it is by no means clear that it is only in primitive societies that ritualistic or symbolic acts can serve a useful social purpose. There is a fairly respectable view, especially espoused by certain psychoanalysts, that the public trial and condemnation of the criminal serves the symbolic function of reinforcing the public sense that there are certain acts that are fundamentally wrong, that must not be done. This view is perhaps most persuasive precisely in those cases where the crime in question does not stir instincts of personal revenge, for the reason that the harm done is to a general, rather than to an individual, interest. Here we may mention particularly 'white collar crimes' such as embezzlement, the sale of influence, and bribery. Under certain social conditions a general deterioration in the moral sense may occur which makes these crimes seem almost innocent.

There are many situations in society where a man – a public official, say, or a corporate executive – must choose among competitors for the same advantage. The corporate purchasing agent, for example, must decide whether to place a profitable supply contract with Acme Manufacturing of Exatronics, Inc.; the public official must choose one among many contenders for appointment to office. In such situations – pervasive in a complex society – there is a natural tendency toward the development of a certain sense of reciprocity between those who

seek advantages and those who control access to them. This
reciprocity may start on a comparatively innocent level as a
mere exchange of social amenities. But it has a strong tendency
to creep towards more tangible forms of expression. What starts
as an exchange of reciprocal esteem may gradually become
an explicit trade of material advantages; what began as an
expression of gratitude for past favours may shift its position
in time by anticipating favours to come. When this anticipation
reaches the explicitness of a bargain we are, of course, confronted with unambiguous bribery.

The usual plea of the bribe-giver or taker is that he only
followed the example he saw everywhere about him, that he
only did directly and candidly what others were doing indirectly
and hypocritically. In such a moral atmosphere, it may be
argued, men need to have their sense of guilt restored; they
must be brought to see that certain things are fundamentally
wrong and that it makes no difference how much company the
criminal has in his wrongdoing. For this purpose 'a ritual act
of expiation' may not be an inappropriate measure.

Before surrendering ourselves to an uncritical enthusiasm for
this function of the criminal law we must recall that the ritual
of expiation loses its whole point if those who perform it do
so with unclean hands. If the agencies of enforcement are
themselves corrupt, if their administration of the law is lax
and favouritistic, then any attempt by them to reanimate the
public sense of sin will serve no purpose but to compound
confusion. Furthermore, the law which furnishes the occasion
for expiation must itself be free from moral taint. It would be
grotesque indeed to select for purposes of moral pedagogy many
statutes in the books today. Take, for example, a price-fixing
law obtained by the retail liquor trade to increase its profits,
but justified on the ground that higher liquor prices will produce
a more sober citizenry, an argument rendered doubly suspect
when it is coupled with a contention that high prices are
necessary to keep the small neighbourhood liquor store in business so that every citizen may have a source of supply at his
elbow. When our statute books are filled with laws like this,
it might be well, before any decision is made to erect a sacri-

ficial altar for the immolation of the lawbreaker, to subject
the House of Law itself to a thorough cleansing and fumigation.

Let us recall at this point that we are now directing our
attention towards possible justifications for a view that attributes
to the criminal law the simple and familiar purpose of punishment, of publicly visiting on the lawbreaker some penalty or
disadvantage. We have considered two such justifications. The
first sees the criminal law as acting in the place of those injured
by the crime and as putting under public control the vengeance
they might otherwise seek outside the forms of law. The other
attributes to the criminal law the task of keeping alive a sense
of guilt, in the words of one psychoanalyst, of providing 'nutri-
ment for the super-ego'. Now neither of these arguments is
likely to have much appeal to those of a strongly rationalistic
and utilitarian bent of mind. Nor is the appeal for those of
such a temperament likely to be enhanced by the fact that
the one argument rests in part on primitive practices, and the
other counts among its staunchest supporters certain disciples
of Freud who give a strongly moralistic flavour to the teachings
of their master.

There is, however, another argument for the retributive
theory, an argument that addresses it appeal to minds of the
most sober and calculative disposition. It consists in shifting
attention from the criminal to the honest man. It may seem
inhumane and brutal to inflict a deliberate hurt on the guilty
man simply because he has hurt another. But what of the law-
abiding man? Is our compassion for the criminal to leave the
honest citizen with no comparative advantage? Is he to gain
nothing by being willing to accept the restraints of law? In
gauging the force of this argument it should be recalled that in
many contexts punishment and reward will appear as opposite
sides of the same coin. Suppose, for example, that a statute
provides that any motorist found guilty of a traffic violation
shall incur a disadvantage by having to pay an increased pre-
mium for his automobile insurance. If an offensive penal
implication is read into this statute, all we have to do to remove
it is to view the statute, not as punishing bad driving, but as
rewarding good driving. So, over the whole spectrum of the

law of crimes, it may be said that it is necessary to maintain a proper balance of advantage between the criminal and the honest man, whether this is done by conferring a reward for law observance or by imposing a penalty for violation of the law. In most contexts it would obviously be impracticable (not to say ludicrous) to confer something like a prize for obeying the law. Hence we are compelled to accomplish this indirectly by imposing a disadvantage on the man found guilty of breaking the law. Unless this is done the scales of justice will weigh out short measure to the man willing to abide by the rules.

So much for the arguments in favour of retaining, as at least *one* of the purposes of the criminal law, the familiar object of punishment. Let us turn now to a purpose that stands at the other extreme from punishment, that of rehabilitation or reform. For just as punishment is often regarded as the most brutal purpose that can be assigned to the criminal law, rehabilitation has generally been considered the most humane.

Now it may seem at first glance as if there were no incompatibility between these two purposes, that they may well supplement each other. It may be said, for example, that there is no reason why the man who is punished by being sent to prison may not, while there, be taught a trade, be given psychiatric help, and generally be put in a condition to meet more adequately the demands of life after his release.

This is not the view generally taken, however, by those who would like to see rehabilitation made the dominant and central concern of the criminal law. They are likely to regard – with some reason – the degradation of punishment as an obstacle to the realization of their ideal. Indeed – and with much less reason – the more radical adherents of the rehabilitative ideal would like to initiate their whole programme by completely purging the administration of the criminal law of any trace of the concept of punishment.

There are good grounds for believing that this cannot be done and should not be attempted. In the first place, there exists nothing at present that can be called a science of rehabilitation. The place such a science would occupy is today a battlefield for contending schools of thought. On this field meet protagonists of behaviouristic, psychoanalytic, mechanistic, and moralistic theories, as well as those who humbly ask only a chance to apply intuitive kindliness. That this conflict of method exists does not mean that nothing has been accomplished. On the contrary, the devotion, skill, and insight of individuals dedicated to the rehabilitative ideal have at times accomplished miracles. But there is as yet no communicable science of rehabilitation, no certain way of measuring the prospects of success in individual cases, and no procedure yielding a confident measure of success.

In this state of the art it is dangerous, indeed, to attempt to eliminate from the law an objective, that of punishment, which at least is familiar and not wholly lacking in rational justification. We should also remember that this objective has built-in limits. While there are no principles by which the appropriate punishments for particular crimes can be exactly set, there are commonsense considerations which suggest, for example, that a life sentence is an inappropriate penalty for a first offence in petty shoplifting. The rehabilitative principle contains no similar intrinsic limitation. From time to time shocking stories come to light of some harmless lunatic originally committed to an asylum for treatment and then kept confined for decades. An uncritical extension of the curative concept over the whole criminal law could easily lead to a multiplication of such incidents many times over.

Such incidents have indeed become much more common than is generally realized. In many states where the question of the sanity of a person accused of crime is raised, there is a procedure for referring to a state psychiatrist or a board of experts the decision whether the accused is 'capable of standing trial'. The assumption here is the wholly reasonable one that a man so deranged that he cannot properly cooperate with his attorney in his own defence is not in fit condition to be tried. If the decision is that he is not capable of standing trial then he may be committed to an insane asylum, where his stay may become indefinite. Furthermore, under the law of many states, if an insane patient presents serious problems of containment and discipline to the asylum, he may be transferred to a regular prison or penitentiary. The ironic result is that a man who if tried and convicted might have had to serve a five-year sentence in prison, ends by spending his entire life in the same prison – waiting until his condition improves sufficiently so that he may be deemed ready for trial.

When we bear in mind that these grotesque happenings are associated with the notion of rehabilitation and cure, we can sense some of the danger that would attend any attempt to supplant, wholesale and overnight, as it were, the objective of punishment with that of cure. A different facet of the problem is revealed when we ask whether this switch in the declared aim of the criminal law would in fact remove the stigma of conviction which adherents of the rehabilitative ideal find so objectionable. Do men in fact feel less shame in being formally declared to be functioning badly than they do in being found to have broken the rules? One perceptive observer has remarked that it is more of an affront to human dignity to subject a man to compulsory improvement than it is to punish him. The truth of this remark may be judged by any parent who will ask himself candidly whether he would rather have his child kept after school for misbehaving or because the child was stupid and needed special after-hours instruction lowered to the level of his capacities.

The most fundamental cleavage between the penal and rehabilitative theories comes to the surface when we ask, 'What circumstances justify a forcible social intervention in the life of the individual?' The answer of the penal theory is fairly clear: 'When the individual has been found to have committed an act defined by the law as a crime. The determination whether he has in fact committed such an act shall be made in a public trial, conducted according to the forms of law.'

Now there are a number of reasons why this mode of determining the need for social intervention should be unsatisfactory to adherents of the rehabilitative ideal. In the first place, a public trial with its dramatic confrontation – sometimes, regrettably, with prosecutor and defence attorney competing for newspaper attention – is scarcely an auspicious beginning for a programme of helping the criminal to adjust to the demands of everyday life. Furthermore, the emphasis placed by the law on the commission of some single act of criminality is itself uncongenial to the rehabilitative theory. From a therapeutic standpoint the commission of a criminal act is only one index among many of the need for curative measures. Even if it could by itself serve as a reliable indication of the need for such measures, those who drafted the statutory table of crimes certainly did not have that purpose in mind. When they decided to attach the brand of criminality to particular acts they may have weighed the damage done to others by the act in question, its propensity to stir imitation, and many other considerations. It is unlikely that they asked themselves whether the act was one which would reliably indicate that curative measures were needed and had some prospect of success. Even if all these difficulties could be resolved, the rehabilitative ideal would still remain unfulfilled as long as the application of curative measures has to await some manifestation of unsocial propensities in outward acts. For the logic of the rehabilitative ideal drives it toward prevention. If crime is the product of certain correctable impulses, it is reasonable to suppose that these impulses must exist in many persons who have as yet had no occasion to express them in overt acts. Why then not take corrective measures before the harm is done? Why not subject the population as a whole to a kind of prophylactic screening to discover who needs to be purged of latent tendencies toward crime?

Surely it requires no argument to demonstrate that any such inquisitorial paternalism could never be tolerated in a free society. Many measures short of so pervasive a surveillance would be equally unacceptable. For example, it is difficult to imagine acceptance of a system under which, instead of trial in open court, a quiet and secluded inquiry by a committee of social scientists would determine whether an individual should be subjected to compulsory detention.

As matters now stand, then, the rehabilitative effort receives into its hands human material that has been 1) branded with the stigma of crime and 2) selected by standards that do not reliably reflect either the need for curative measures or their prospective success. This is a situation with which the more ardent supporters of the rehabilitative ideal can hardly be expected to be happy. Yet what is involved is not a repudiation of the rehabilitative ideal, but a compromise to which that ideal must submit in the interest of freedom, human dignity, and due process. At present this compromise costs more than it should. In particular the criminal trial as it is now often conducted is unworthy of any ideal that could be ascribed to the criminal law. But with all allowance for improvement here and elsewhere in the administration of the law, some element of compromise between divergent goals must remain.

In other words, for the foreseeable future the rehabilitative and penal theories are condemned to live in an uneasy alliance from which neither can fully escape. As with an unhappy marriage where effective action has been excluded, the resulting frustration has tended to take itself out in words.

So we find adherents of the rehabilitative ideal attempting to rewrite the whole vocabulary of the criminal law in terms more congenial to its objectives. A draft code recently prepared for one of the new nations undertook a complete revision of the terminology of crime. The code itself was designated not as a Penal or Criminal Code, but as a Code of Correction. Arrest became a 'taking into temporary custody'. Crime itself was defined not as an offence against the law, but as 'a condition subject to correction'. How little is likely to be accomplished by such changes in nomenclature can be seen if we weigh the present connotations of expressions like 'reformatory' and 'house of correction' against the hopes that must have accompanied the original coinage of those terms.

The attempt to rewrite the criminal law in softer words may be attributed to laudable motives and may seem, in any event, relatively harmless. This impulse is far from harmless, however, when it extends to the definition of crime itself. When that definition is softened up beyond a certain degree, then the meaning of due process of law has been destroyed. One of the guiding principles of the rehabilitative ideal is that of 'flexibility'. Its object is to treat not the act, but the man, and every man is to some extent a special case. This view, with proper qualifications, has much to recommend it when it relates to the policy to be pursued *after conviction*. Matters stand quite otherwise, however, when the policy of flexibility is extended to the definition of crime itself. If the words used to state when a man is guilty of a criminal act, and when he is not, are loosely put together, then guarantees of fair trial become meaningless. One cannot measure out just treatment with a yardstick made of rubber.

Nor is the renaming of things always wholly innocent when it relates to matters other than the definition of crime. Imprisonment, by whatever name it is called, is a harsh thing, and the discipline that must be exercised over human beings in close confinement can never be wholly agreeable to those subject to it. When an attempt is made to hide the harsh realities of criminal justice behind euphemistic descriptions, a corrupting irony may be introduced into ordinary speech that is fully as frightening as Orwell's 'Newspeak'. A perceptive observer, reporting on a visit to an institution for boys with behaviour difficulties, recounts the following incident: one of the boys who had broken some disciplinary rule was 'required to stand before a wall while a seventy-pound fire hose was played on his back. This procedure went under the name of "hydrotherapy".' That this ironic renaming is not entirely a modern invention is shown by an expression of long standing, 'the water cure'. This expression in turn has its ugly cousin in the familiar, 'That'll teach you!' which so often accompanies acts of sheer retaliation.

In seeking the proper place for the rehabilitative ideal in the total administration of criminal justice, we must not imagine that the realization of this ideal will in practice be entrusted to a few perceptive and kindly social scientists. The person subjected to curative measures will inevitably have his chief and most intimate contact with attendants and caretakers, who will be ordinary human beings, subject to ordinary human frailties. If these persons are assigned a function they do not understand and are forced to employ a vocabulary foreign to their actual motives, then hypocrisy, ineptitude, and some measure of cruelty are inevitable. For it seems almost a law of human nature that when a man is compelled to act out a role in which he has no real belief, the result will be to bring out his worst qualities.

Before quitting the subject of rehabilitation, it might be well to remind the reader once again that there are many different kinds of crimes to be found listed in the statutes. There is a tendency in discussions about the theory or purpose of the criminal law to speak in terms of 'crime' in general, and what lies in the back of the mind are the most obvious acts of violence, like murder and rape. But it is not crimes like these that form the longest chapters of the criminal code. As for rehabilitation, there would, for example, be a considerable incongruity, to say the least, if the convicted president of a huge corporation were turned over to a board of psychiatrists to be cured of the bad habit of violating the antitrust laws. When we speak of curing a man of a tendency towards crime, we must not forget what diverse activities make up the catalogue of modern crimes.

There remain for brief treatment the two remaining functions or 'theories' of the criminal law: deterrence and prevention.

Plainly there is no fundamental incompatibility between the penal theory and the objective of deterrence. Scholars debate the question whether the threat of punishment actually does deter. Stories are told of the days of public hangings in England when a man might be hanged for a great variety of minor offences, including theft. It is said that pickpockets found in such occasions an excellent opportunity for plying their trade, especially during the time when the actual hanging was taking place and all eyes were on the dangling figure at the end of the rope. Ironically, that figure was himself not uncommonly a convicted pickpocket.

Whatever moral may be derived from such stories, common sense tells us that the fear of punishment must in some measure, and for some persons, act as a deterrent to crime. A system of criminal law based on punishment will as a matter of course furnish this deterrence as a kind of by-product. There is, therefore, no fundamental incompatibility between the penal and deterrent theories.

One thing is perfectly clear, and that is that no civilized system of criminal law could take as its *exclusive* aim that of deterrence. This would mean that when an individual was found to have committed a criminal act, what would happen to him would have no relation to his deserts, but would be judged solely by its effect on others. It is, of course, quite true that during a real or supposed 'crime wave' the sentences meted out will tend to be somewhat more severe than under ordinary conditions. In this way the objective of deterrence may enter into and give a special direction to the administration of the law. But this is a very different matter from making deterrence the chief or sole objective of the criminal law. No one could seriously recommend that when something goes wrong, and we cannot identify the culprit, we revert to the old practice of executing every tenth man.

With respect to the theory of *prevention* there is, again, ordinarily no fundamental incompatibility between it and the familiar objective of punishment. Most modern forms of punishment (in contrast with the ducking stool and the whipping post) serve to take the criminal out of society for a period and during that time preclude him from a repetition of his offence.

This does not mean that the administration of the law can disregard prevention as a separate objective and simply assume that it will be achieved through a system oriented towards the objectives of a penal theory. For one thing there is the well-known fact that during his imprisonment a criminal often picks up from his more experienced fellow prisoners skills that will serve his criminal career when he is released. Though this possibility raises some difficult questions of prison administration, it suggests no fundamental tension between the objectives of punishment and prevention.

As with the objective of deterrence, it is difficult to imagine a system of criminal law *exclusively* devoted to prevention. There is, however, one branch of the criminal law that approaches that orientation. This is found in laws having to do with what are called sexual psychopaths. If it were possible to cure such persons of their dangerous tendencies, their situation would present a powerful argument for supplanting punishment with a system exclusively devoted to curative measures. Unfortunately it is by no means clear that their condition can be cured. If it cannot, then, when we remember, for example, the psychic scars little children can receive from their advances or attacks, a good case can be made for removing psychopaths to a safe distance from society – indefinitely. But, here again, problems of fairness and due process arise to complicate the problem. Must such a person, before being put away, be convicted of crime, or is it enough that psychiatrists regard him as a potential danger? A clear-cut answer to questions of this sort is precluded by the fact that our knowledge of such conditions is still imperfect and what purports to be an answer given in the name of science is often no more than a reasonably informed guess. With matters in this state we are not yet ready to effect a final resolution among conflicting theories of the criminal law and here, as elsewhere, must be content with a kind of uneasy compromise.

Laws and legal institutions characteristically serve more than one purpose

In the lengthy discussion of the ends of the criminal law just concluded, we began, it should be recalled, by asking ourselves whether the criminal law could not be clarified, and its rules made more certain, by assigning to it a single purpose, rather than a multiplicity of purposes. We concluded that this could not be done. Furthermore, to adopt for the whole of the criminal law a single objective would distort and brutalize it. This is certainly so with respect to the unresolved tension between the penal and rehabilitative ideals. To pursue the objective of punishment so rigorously as to exclude even the hope or possibility of rehabilitation would reduce the criminal law to a savage expression of the instinct for retaliation. On the other hand, rehabilitation divorced from any concern to mete out to each his due, released from legal restraints to search out among the population apt subjects for its unwelcome attentions – this would be something intolerable in a free society.

We are now ready to deal with a broader question: Is it true of law generally that its rules and institutions characteristically serve a multiplicity of purposes? The answer must be in the affirmative.

Let us turn to a body of law as remote as possible from that concerned with crimes. As every layman knows there are rules of law stating what formalities must be followed in order to make some act legally effective; a last will and testament, for example, may require the presence of two or more witnesses who must sign the document attesting that they were present when the testator affixed his signature. Again, certain contracts are not valid unless put in writing and signed by the contracting party.

What is the purpose of such formalities? A complete answer would require a lengthy analysis and would lead us far afield. We may, however, safely discern two principal purposes, each quite distinct from the other. *First*, the purpose of these rules is to ensure that the transaction will be recorded and preserved in a trustworthy form. It would be most unfortunate, for example, if the distribution of a man's estate should depend upon a recollection of oral statements made by him during his life, not to speak of the invitation to fraud that would be presented if such a loose way of establishing his intentions were given legal effect. *Second*, requirements of formality are also imposed to bring home to the party the significance of what he is doing. Many a person willing to make casual statements about his intentions of future generosity would stop, reflect, and perhaps draw back if he were asked to put those statements down in writing. The law needs, in other words, to set up a clear finish line for the expression of legal intention.

A given formality may serve one of these purposes well, the other badly. This is true of what is called the holographic will. In some jurisdictions a will written, dated, and signed in the hand of the testator is valid without more. Such a requirement of form serves reasonably well the object of securing a relatively foolproof memorial of the testor's intention. On the other hand, being consummated in private and consisting, perhaps, of a paragraph inserted in a long and informal letter, it serves very badly the objective of bringing home to the testator a full realization of the importance and significance of his act. In states where the holographic will is legally valid, the courts are constantly plagued with the problem of drawing a line between expressions that are definitely 'testamentary' and those that merely record some passing hope or expectation.

Uncertainty as to the precise purpose served by a requirement of form often embarrasses the interpretation of statutory requirements of form. In many legal systems the promise of a surety (one who guarantees the payment of a debt owed by another) is required to be in writing. Now requirements of this sort are often rather loosely construed by the courts; if the circumstances offer a sufficient protection against the dangers sought to be avoided by the requirement of a writing, the requirement may be dispensed with. Suppose that, although the alleged undertaking to be surety was wholly oral, the proof indicates that the alleged surety was paid and accepted a sum of money for his undertaking. Does this suffice to make his promise binding? If the object of the requirement of a writing is to warn the party that he is crossing over from casual talk into the area of legal liability, then the acceptance of a payment will serve much the same purpose as a signed writing. On the other hand, if the purpose of the requirement of a writing is to secure a reliable memorial of the terms of the undertaking – what debts were included, how long a period was covered, and the like – then proof that a payment was accepted is a less satisfactory substitute for the signed writing, though it should not be thought that it is wholly irrelevant to that purpose, since the amount paid and accepted gives some indication as to the nature of the transaction.

In cases like this the tension between opposing purposes served by the same legal rule presents a relatively undisturbing complication. Its implications can scarcely be compared with those introduced by the conflict between the penal and rehabilitative ideals in the criminal law. Nevertheless it is useful to keep in mind that problems caused by the fact that legal rules and institutions characteristically serve a multiplicity of ends are ubiquitous, and that they introduce what may be called a permanent dilemma into the administration of the law.

Indeed, there lies in the concept of justice itself a hidden conflict or tension between opposing conceptions of the end sought by justice. On the one hand, there is what has been called *legal* justice, a justice which demands that we stick by the announced rules and not make exceptions in favour of particular individuals, a justice which conceives that men should live under the same 'rule of law' and be equally bound by its terms. On the other hand, there is the justice of *dispensation*, a justice ready to make exceptions when the established rules work unexpected hardship in particular cases, a justice ready to bend the letter of the law to accomplish a fair result.

Let us see how these two conceptions can come into conflict in the decision of actual cases. Let us suppose a statute that is concerned with the hazards created by icy sidewalks in the winter-time. The statute proceeds on the assumption that it should be the responsibility of the home-owner to keep the sidewalks leading into his house in a reasonably safe condition for tradesmen and visitors who may have occasion to use them. To that end it imposes on the home-owner a liability to respond in damages for any injury received because his sidewalks are left in an icy condition – a liability which he can, of course, forfend by scraping the ice off or sprinkling it with sand or ashes. The statute provides that no suit may be brought under it unless the home-owner either knew of the injury when it occurred or was notified within ten days by the injured party of the fact and circumstances of his injury. The reason for this requirement is fairly apparent. In freezing weather, and particularly during a period when there are alternate freezes and thaws, it is very difficult to recall, and virtually impossible to prove, what the condition of a sidewalk was, let us say, a month in the past. The liability imposed on the owner is a stringent one and he ought not to be exposed to groundless or trumped-up claims which he is not in a position to disprove.

Let us suppose that Mr X, a house-to-house canvasser, claims

that on 10 February he slipped and sprained his ankle on Mr
Y's sidewalk because it was covered with ice. Y was, however,
absent at the time, and is first told of the injury on 5 May,
when X calls with a lawyer and threatens suit. By the terms
of the statute, X's claim is barred. X claims, however, that he
was preoccupied with business problems, that there was illness
in his home, that after the injury he limped badly, that Y's
home was hard to reach, that he did not know the telephone
number or street address, and generally that it would have been
difficult and inconvenient for him to give the required notice.
Here rather plainly the court is bound to apply the statute as
written. Indeed one might cite a surprising authority in support
of this conclusion, for it was Sigmund Freud who wrote that
justice 'demands that a law once made will not be broken in
favour of an individual'.

One may imagine a series of cases arising in which the ex-
cuse for failing to give the required notice becomes increasingly
persuasive, until, at the end of the spectrum, we encounter the
case in which the injured party did not give the notice because
his fall knocked him unconscious and he remained in that
condition for twelve days after his fall. Here we are apt to
revolt against the letter of the law. Surely, we may say, the
statute should not be so construed that the injured man will
never, at any moment of time, acquire a claim he can effectively
assert. At this juncture we are apt to feel that we must abandon
legal justice – the law must be the same for all – in favour of the
justice of *dispensation* – the law must not itself become an instrument of injustice. But just where is the dividing line? There
is and can be no easy answer to this question.

The 'human element' in law

Summarizing our conclusions, we may say that there are two
pervasive problems – they might also be called *permanent* problems – of the law. There is first the problem of keeping the
various institutions and official roles that make up a legal
system in accord with one another; second, there are the
ambiguities and uncertainties introduced by the fact that legal

rules and legal institutions characteristically serve a multiplicity of ends.

Now to each of these problems there is an obvious and drastic answer. To the first problem there is the answer: Put the whole legal system under a firm chain of command so that each level of the system is answerable to the level immediately above it. To the second problem there is the answer: Eliminate uncertainties by assigning to each legal rule and to each legal institution a single, clear-cut purpose.

We have tried to show how disastrous it would be if either of these 'obvious' answers were adopted, or rather, if a serious attempt were made to act upon either of them. Once these simplistic remedies are rejected, it becomes apparent that the successful functioning of a legal system depends upon repeated acts of human judgement at every level of the system. Once this ineluctable necessity is accepted, it becomes apparent how foolish it is to suppose that the failings of a legal system can all be attributed to the 'human elements'.

The human element can of course fail, and it can fail not simply because of corruption or sloth, but for lack of a sense of institutional role and a failure to perceive the true nature of the problems involved in constructing and administering a legal system. But if the human element is a possible source of failure, it is also an indispensable ingredient in any just and humane legal system. The complex undertaking we call 'law' requires at every turn the exercise of judgement, and that judgement must be exercised by human beings for human beings. It cannot be built into a computer.

Part 2

The Sources of Law

Introduction

The term 'sources of law' is ordinarily used in a much narrower sense than will be attributed to it here. In the literature of jurisprudence the problem of 'sources' relates to the question: Where does the judge obtain the rules by which to decide cases? In this sense, among the sources of law will commonly be listed: statutes, judicial precedents, custom, the opinion of experts, morality, and equity. In the usual discussions these various sources of law are analysed and some attempt is made to state the conditions under which each can appropriately be drawn upon in the decision of legal controversies. Curiously, when a legislature is enacting law we do not talk about the 'sources' from which it derives its decision as to what the law shall be, though an analysis in these terms might be more enlightening than one directed toward the more restricted function performed by the judge.

Our concern here will be with 'sources' in a much broader sense than is usual in the literature of jurisprudence. Our interest is not so much in sources of laws, as in sources of law. From whence does the law generally draw not only its content but its force in men's lives?

This problem is, of course, intimately connected with the ancient debate between two opposing schools of legal philosophy, that of legal positivism and that of natural law. We shall have occasion later to relate that familiar controversy to the analysis which will be presented here. Meanwhile, the reader acquainted with it is asked to put the issue of 'positivism' versus 'the law of nature' to one side and to participate, for the time being, in a somewhat different kind of inquiry. This will relate to a distinction between 'made' law and 'implicit' law.

Made law and implicit law

To serve as our prototype for *made law* we shall take the *statute*; our corresponding model standing for *implicit law* will be *customary law*. As our discussion progresses it will become apparent that neither of these is in fact what could be called a pure type; in the statute there is always an element of implicit law, while some element of enactment or conscious creation enters into the rules of customary law. For the time being we shall ignore these complications and present the two forms of law as if they stood, without qualification, for contrasting, pure types.

First, then, let us turn to the *statute* as exemplifying those qualities that characterize *made law*. A statute derives from a determinate human source. It is enacted by the decision of a legislator or a legislative body. It comes into being at a determinate time; it carries a date which tells us precisely when it became effective and marks off the time in the past when it did not yet exist. Its terms are to be found in the words of the statute itself. If we want to know what those words mean, we look first at the words themselves and not at some expression of a more or less equivalent thought to be found somewhere else in the literature of the law.

In contrast with the statute, *customary law* may be said to exemplify *implicit law*. Let us, therefore, describe customary law in terms that will reveal to the maximum this quality of implicitness. A custom is not declared or enacted, but grows or develops through time. The date when it first came into full effect can usually be assigned only within broad limits. Though we may be able to describe in general the class of persons among whom the custom has come to prevail as a standard of conduct, it has no definite author; there is no person or defined human agency we can praise or blame for its being good or bad. There is no authoritative verbal declaration of the terms of the custom; it expresses itself not in a succession of words, but in a course of conduct.

Customary law can be viewed as being implicit law in a double sense. In the first place, the rules of customary law are not first brought into being and then projected upon the conduct they are intended to regulate. They find their implicit expression in the conduct itself. In the second place, the *purpose* of such rules never comes to explicit expression. A statute may contain a preamble explaining the evil it was intended to avert or the good it was designed to promote. There is nothing like this in customary law. We have to infer what its rules sought to accomplish. We have to assume that these rules arose from some need felt by those who first shaped their conduct by them. If we seek to understand what that need might be, we must place ourselves in the situation of the parties affected and infer why it was they found it appropriate to impose the patterns they did on their actions toward one another.

The contention that will be advanced here is that many of the disputes of legal philosophy hinge upon an undeclared preference between made law and implicit law. We shall have occasion later to probe the fundamental motives that may lie back of such a preference. For the moment let us examine an historical instance of the way in which one famous advocate of made law – that is, one who preferred that all law be made law – was able to convert what was plainly implicit law into terms more congenial to his system.

John Austin was that advocate of made law. His famous Lectures on Jurisprudence, first published in outline form in *The Province of Jurisprudence Determined*, (1832), have had an enormous influence on legal thinking in the Anglo-American countries, an influence that extends, one is tempted to say *especially* extends, to those who have not in fact read Austin. It will be instructive to see how Austin absorbs customary law into his system, a system which presupposes that all law ought to be, and in fact is, what we have here called made law.

For Austin all laws consist, directly or mediately, of rules laid down by a sovereign power enjoying the habit of obedience within a given society. The statute, enacted by legislative authority, fits this model neatly and without apparent friction. The judge's role is absorbed with somewhat more difficulty. This is especially so in the English system where much law had its origin in judicial decisions and was not derived even remotely from statutory enactments. The curious fact is that in 'making' this law the judges never talked as if they were making anything at all, but as though they were merely applying a law already implicit in previous law or in the nature of human society. Austin's solution was to disregard the judges' talk and to brand their 'finding' of law as the making of law. We shall have occasion to examine later some of the distortions produced by this forcing of judge-made law into an uncomfortable mould.

For the time being we shall concern ourselves with the much more drastic distortions that resulted from Austin's attempt to convert customary law into a form of state-made law. In the decision of controversies, courts in all legal systems often derive the rules they apply from customary practices that have grown up quite outside any context of enacted law. This is especially apt to be the case in commercial disputes. Where 'the custom of merchants' was taken by judges as the standard of decision, the judges spoke of this custom as having the force of law and they applied it as something binding on them as well as on the parties. If this view of the matter were accepted, a very considerable breach would be opened in any system of thought which insists that all law is made law and that law never can, or does, just 'grow'.

Austin's solution for this difficulty is expressed in the following passages:

At its origin, a custom is a rule of conduct which the governed observe spontaneously.... The custom is transmuted into positive law, when it is adopted as such by the courts of justice, and when the judicial decisions fashioned upon it are enforced by the power of the state. But before it is adopted by the courts, and clothed with the legal sanction, it is merely a rule ... generally observed by the citizens or subjects; but deriving the only force, which it can be said to possess, from the general disapprobation falling on those who transgress it.... The admirers of customary law love to trick out their idol with mysterious and imposing attributes. But ... there is nothing of mystery about it ... considered as moral rules turned into positive laws, customary laws are established by the state ...*

* *Lectures on Jurisprudence*, vol. i, 4th ed., John Murray, Ltd., London, 1879, pp. 104–5.

Austin's treatment of custom involves something like a doctrine of second birth: custom starts as a kind of conventional
morality and is then reborn as law when it is adopted as a
standard of decision by the act of a court. There are a number
of artificialities concealed in this apparently innocent – if ten-
dentious – interpretation. In the first place, as we have already
intimated, this is not the way the courts themselves look on the
matter. It is true that not every customer practice will be
accepted as a standard of judicial decision. Some customs are
injurious to the public interest or are contrary to legislative
enactments. The courts will, accordingly, scrutinize the implications of a custom before accepting it as law. Nevertheless,
when this acceptance takes place the courts do not think of
themselves as *enacting*, but rather as *recognizing*, law. There
are situations in which a custom is so obviously fair and beneficial that no doubt will arise but that it would, in case of
controversy, be accepted by the courts as a source of law. The
outcome of litigation may be so foreseeable that litigation
will not take place. In such a situation the result of Austin's
analysis is to deny the name of law to custom precisely in those
situations in which it is so plainly law that no legal test of its
right to that designation will be likely to occur.

Secondly, Austin's interpretation would lead us to suppose
that when a second case arises the court deciding this case
would look not to the custom itself, but to the authoritative
statement of the effect of the custom contained in the first
decision. But in practice this will seldom occur. Usually the
second case will involve some slightly different facet of the
custom, one not directly involved in the first case. The second
court will, accordingly, derive its standard of decision from the
custom itself, and not from the words used by the first court
in attempting to describe the custom.

Thirdly, customs have a habit of changing through time.
Changes may come about through altered external conditions,
because of technological progress, or as indirect accommodation to new forms of enacted law. However the changes occur,
they are likely to be recognized and accepted in later judicial
decisions. Here the doctrine of rebirth becomes, in effect, a

doctrine of continuous rebirth, with all the embarrassments such a view entails for any notion that a custom is in some way wholly transmuted into a radically different thing on the date when it was first used by a court to decide a litigated issue.

Fourthly and lastly, if we reject all the qualifications just made, and accept Austin's doctrine of rebirth on its own terms, there remains an element of implicit law in the doctrine itself. Austin plainly assumes that once a custom has been accepted by a court as a standard of decision, that acceptance holds good, but simply for the case at hand, but for all similar cases in the future. This is because Austin takes for granted the existence of a rule or practice – a *custom* – by which courts will follow their own prior decisions. Now this rule was never 'made' by any explicit enactment; it is a part of the customary rules governing the actions of courts. Like most customary rules it has its fringes of uncertainty and is subject to exceptions in instances that cannot be clearly defined in advance. So that, in the end, the security of the custom reborn as enacted law against a relapse into its unbaptized state depends itself upon a custom implicit in the practice of courts.

The way in which Austin remade customary law to conform to an image more to his own liking is by no means an isolated phenomenon. It is symptomatic of a struggle that goes on all the time in legal philosophy to recast material presenting itself in an unwelcome form into something more congenial to the philosopher's preconceptions of what law ought to be. But just as Austin sought to remake implicit law into made law, so there are philosophers who seek to unmake made law into something closer to implicit law.

We are all familiar with the view that statutes and enactments are transitory things; the reality of law in the long run, it is said, lies in public acceptance. Statutes that run counter to generally accepted notions of what is right may never really come into effect for lack of enforcement. If some attempt is made for a while to enforce them, they will tend to die out through public resistance, or the growing indifference of prosecutors, or because the courts gradually find ways of whittling them down to insignificance by restrictive interpretations. There are philosophers who, far from deploring this state of affairs, welcome it. For them the law is not something handed out like a press release at ten o'clock in the morning. In their view the living law – the *real* law – grows and shapes itself silently in response to the felt needs of those who are subject to it.

As a counterweight to Austin, let us at this point quote from a modern legal sociologist:

From what source does the law derive? For sociological theory ... that question permits of only one answer ... the law derives from the social group; legal rules express the way in which the group considers that social relations ought to be ordered. This point of view is quite different from that generally taught. The current doctrine ... does not bring to clear articulation the question of the origin of the force of law generally, though that question is basic and fundamental. Instead the current doctrine applies its efforts to the different modalities in which the law appears (legislation, custom, judicial decisions, expert opinion), thus giving the impression that these modalities are radically different from one another. On the contrary, from a sociological point of view, these formal sources of law, which the jurists are concerned to distinguish, are simply different varieties of one single and unique source: the will of the social group. Besides parting from the current doctrine in the way just indicated, I also differ from it in attaching a very great importance to custom ...

Statutory law is not essentially different from custom: both are the expressions of the will of the group. That which distinguishes them is a certain given technique: while ... custom is spontaneous and 'unconscious', statutory law proceeds from a specialized organ and originates by means of a procedure ... called enactment ...

The question has been raised as to which of the two systems – that of custom or that of statutory law – should be preferred. In a famous controversy in Germany at the beginning of the nineteenth century two jurists, Savigny and Thibaut, joined issue on that question. The first was a supporter of custom, the second a supporter of statutory law. Savigny ... discerned the proper view, confirmed by contemporary sociology, according to which law is the product of the collective conscience.*

* Henri Lévy-Bruhl, *Sociologie du droit*, Presses Universitaires, Paris, 1961, pp. 39–40, 55, and 57.

The author goes on to say that Savigny, though correct in his fundamental conception of law, was mistaken in believing that custom did not need the aid of legislation. The author points out that though custom in its origins may represent a more direct expression of the collective conscience, it has the failing that it tends to become rigid and unresponsive to new conditions. When this occurs, it needs to be supplemented and limbered up by legislation.

The contrasting viewpoints found in Austin and Lévy-Bruhl express a conflict that is pervasive and perennial in legal philosophy. We shall not attempt here to say which of these viewpoints is 'right'. Rather our endeavour will be to render to each its duet. In accomplishing this objective we shall have occasion to make distinctions that are commonly ignored when an issue is joined, as it often is, in either-or terms.

So far we have taken customary law as our prototype of implicit law. In what follows we shall have occasion to broaden our conception of that kind of law. To take a homely example, suppose a group of friends embark on a camping trip. They take with them tents, portable beds, food, and equipment for cooking their meals. Characteristically such a group will soon discover that there is implicit in their undertaking a need for some division of function and for certain more or less formal rules declaring the duties incumbent on the different members of the party. If there is among the group an experienced camper with a natural gift for organization, it may well be that the need for order within the group will be set largely – though not entirely – by his informal law-making. In the absence of such a commanding figure, the needed order may, with many false starts and much fumbling, come into being by a kind of spontaneous growth, though the course of that development may at certain critical points be shaped by explicit decisions, either by individuals or by something like a majority vote. In the 'law' of the group that thus comes to govern their actions, a large ingredient will be implicit in the demands of the common enterprise on which they have embarked. This implicit law is not something wholly distinct from and set over against the 'made' elements in the order they achieve, but enters into a kind of silent partnership with those elements to provide a rounded system or order for the essential activities of the group. So in what follows we shall generally speak of 'implicit law' as an element of a larger system that is in part consciously 'made' or brought into being by enactment.

Our illustration of the camping trip may also serve as a warning that in what follows we shall be forced to use the word 'law' in a somewhat broader sense than is common today. In modern usage 'law' has come to be so closely identified with 'made law' that any other employment of the term is likely to be branded as an abuse. This restricted conception of 'law' may be said to make its own distinctive contributions both to clarity and to obfuscation. It cannot, however, serve our purposes when we are attempting to distinguish the made and implicit elements that join to produce a functioning system of legal rules. Still less can it be useful in the historical discussion that immediately follows, for the history of law is in large part the story of a shift from a view of law that sees it as intrinsic to the needs of group life to one that sees it as the result of deliberate enactment.

The role of implicit law and made law in legal history

The account that follows will be largely based on what still remains the most famous single work in legal anthropology, Sir Henry Sumner Maine's *Ancient Law: Its Connection with the Early History of Society and Its Relation to Modern Ideas* (first published in 1861). In the first and second chapters of that work, Maine discerns six stages in the development of law. These stages mark way stations on the long and tortuous route by which mankind finally, and one is tempted to say, reluctantly, arrived at the conclusion that law can be made. This final stage Maine designates as that of *Legislation*.

There is much that is today unacceptable in Maine's account. He seems mistakenly to assume that every society passes through certain stages of development in the same order. He largely ignores the influence of economic factors. He indulges in hazardous conjectures about prehistorical times. The sources on which a study like Maine's might draw have today been expanded many times over, not only by the discovery of ancient codes unknown to Maine but by systematic studies of contemporary primitive societies – studies that were in Maine's time in their infancy.

With all its limitations, we can still learn much from Maine's account if we cease to worry ourselves about its literal accuracy and treat it as a kind of allegory, full of insight into the processes by which law grows. In what follows we shall preserve the general outlines of Maine's analysis. In order to avoid digressions into the Roman and Greek sources on which Maine drew, we shall introduce some changes in nomenclature. Our rendition of Maine's account of the first two stages will have to be 'free' in ways that go beyond nomenclature. The necessity for this interpretive licence arises from the fact that scholars are in disagreement as to just what Maine meant by his first and second stages. To avoid a tedious exercise in exegesis, we shall simply present our own interpretation of what Maine meant, even if this requires some rewriting of what he said.

In its most primitive manifestations law is seen as something that displays itself much as the forces of nature display themselves. In Maine's words it is 'in the air' and '... in the infancy of mankind, no sort of legislature, not even a distinct author of law, is contemplated or conceived of'.

Maine might have gone on to point out, as many anthropologists have since his time, that in the earliest and most primitive condition of society, many distinctions taken today as a matter of course did not even rise to the level of consciousness. Among the rules by which human conduct shapes itself we would distinguish those of morality, of law, of religion, of etiquette, and of technology. The primitive mind found little occasion to make such distinctions. 'This is how you catch fish; this is how you ward off evil; this is how you transfer the right to do a sacred dance' – precepts like these were all thought of as being on the same footing. All served simply to describe 'the way things are'. All were, in our terms, implicit law.

When disputes were decided by a judge, priest, or chieftain, it is unlikely that anyone would think of his act as the *making* of law. It probably would not even be thought of as the *applying* of law, but rather as a simple discernment – perhaps inspired by supernatural forces – of 'the way things are'.

Such is, then – with some liberties of interpretation – Maine's conception of the first stage in the development of law.

His second stage is that of *Customary Law*. By this term he meant approximately what is meant by it in ordinary speech. But a difficulty at once arises: What is the difference between the second stage, that of customary law, and the first stage, when law is thought of simply 'as the way things are'? Is custom itself not 'blind'? Is it not true that people follow custom simply because 'this is the way things are'?

The difference Maine had in mind was this: In the second stage the fact that some mode of conduct has become customary is regarded as a *reason* for following it. In the first stage, in Maine's own words, 'Law has scarcely reached the footing of custom; it is rather a habit.' In the stage of customary law, on the other hand, men have become aware, however dimly, of the fact that there may be an alternative to the ways in which they have acted in the past. In instances where there is some element of choice in their conformity, they may follow custom because of a perception of the need for shared and accepted rules of conduct and a realization that a departure from established rules would act disruptively. Plainly in this sense of choice, however restricted it may be, there is the first germ of the notion that law can be deliberately made.

As society becomes more complex, the body of customary rules inevitably expands; with the expansion the likelihood of conflicts within the system increases. There thus arises a need for someone to keep track of the rules and to provide authoritative interpretations in cases of doubt. In many societies, including the Roman, this need is met by a class of priests or learned men who serve as the official custodians and interpreters of custom. The functions of this class will normally give to it an aristocratic and exclusive quality. So long as the society remains preliterate, however, any discontents aroused by this special position of privilege are likely to be stilled by a perception of its necessity.

With the invention and spread of writing, the matter assumes a different complexion. The monopoly of knowledge that previously served a useful social purpose may cease to do so. There may be demands that the law be made generally known. When these demands acquire a sufficient force, in Maine's words, 'We arrive at the era of Codes, those ancient codes of which the Twelve Tables of Rome were the most famous specimen ... laws engraven on tablets and published to the people take the place of usages deposited with the recollection of a privileged oligarchy ... [The value of these codes] did not consist in any approach to symmetrical classification, or to terseness and clearness of expression, but in their publicity, and in the knowledge which they furnished to everybody, as to what he was to do, and what not to do.'*

These codes were not legislative enactments in the modern sense, but were thought of primarily as a reduction to writing of the rules already established by custom. But plainly once such codes became familiar, another step had been taken along the lengthy road that leads to an explicit recognition that laws can be made. Even in the Twelve Tables there was, apparently, more innovation than Maine appreciated. It is evident, in any case, that the mere reduction to formal written expression of rules previously unsystematized could not but introduce some changes in substance. And to the extent that such changes were recognized, men's minds were opened up to the possibility that more extensive and deliberate changes might be made.

Maine himself thus describes the significance of the Codes in legal history:

When primitive law has once been embodied in a Code, there is an end to what may be called its spontaneous development. Henceforward the changes effected in it, if effected at all, are effected deliberately and from without. It is impossible to suppose that the customs of any race or tribe remained unaltered during the whole of the long – in some cases the immense – interval between their

* *Ancient Law* with notes by Sir Frederick Pollock, John Murray, Ltd., London, 1912, pp. 12–13.

declaration [that is, their *discernment and* declaration] by a patri-
archal monarch and their publication in writing. It would be unsafe
too to affirm that no part of the alteration was effected deliberately.
But from the little we know of the progress of law during this
period, we are justified in assuming that set purpose had the very
smallest share in producing change. Such innovations on the earliest
usages as disclose themselves appear to have been dictated by
feelings and modes of thought which, under our present mental
conditions, we are unable to comprehend. A new era begins, however, with the Codes. Wherever, after this epoch, we trace the
course of legal modification we are able to attribute it to the conscious desire of improvement, or at all events of compassing objects
other than those which were aimed at in the primitive times.*

In Maine's analysis the first step toward explicit legislation,
following the era of Codes, did not take the form of an open
declaration of new law. Rather, it introduced legal reform under
the cover of fictions. In Maine's own account:

... I employ the expression 'Legal Fiction' to signify any assumption which conceals, or affects to conceal, the fact that a rule of
law has undergone alteration, its letter remaining unchanged, its
operation being modified. ... It is not difficult to understand why
fictions in all their forms are particularly congenial to the infancy
of society. They satisfy the desire for improvement, which is not
quite wanting, at the same time that they do not offend the superstitious disrelish for change which is always present. At a particular stage of social progress they are invaluable expedients for over-
coming the rigidity of law, and, indeed, without one of them, the
Fiction of Adoption which permits the family tie to be artificially
created, it is difficult to understand how society would ever have
escaped from its swaddling-clothes, and taken its first steps towards
civilization.†

In speaking of the special significance of the fiction of adoption, Maine had in mind that it was the family expanded by
that fiction which furnished the model, and in some cases the
actual historical forerunner, of the larger political units that
came to characterize later societies.

The legal fiction is often thought of as a kind of clumsy, self-

* *Ancient Law*, p. 26.
† ibid., pp. 30–31.

deluding kind of legislation. There are overtones of this view in Maine himself, as the quoted passages indicate. This view of the fiction is, however, unjust and distorts the role it has actually played in the development of the law. One of the perennial problems of legislative reform is to fit changes into established law so that they will not clash with those parts of the legal system that remain unaltered. With all our carefully compiled statute books and elaborate indexes, modern legislators often fail to foresee points of rub between their innovations and the body of law against which they are projected. The modern legislature, with a broad competence in lawmaking, is in a position to correct these oversights with curative legislation. No such resource was available in primitive society. Its legislation was of necessity piecemeal for there existed no broad competence in lawmaking. In such a situation the legal reformer acts wisely when he gives to his innovations a form that will facilitate their absorption into the existing law. The legal fiction probably owes its origin, then, not so much to a superstitious disrelish for change or some instinct for self-deceit, as to an impulse toward harmony and system. By giving to the new law the verbal form of the old it facilitated its absorption into the existing corpus of rules.

The next and fifth stage in Maine's account involves, or may involve, a much broader reform of the law than that permitted by the legal fiction. We now encounter for the first time the notion that legal reform may be guided by some transcendent model, some ideal legal system to which, it is thought, all laws ought to conform. Typically this ideal legal system will be located historically in the past. The notion of a lost perfection, of a fall from former grace, is one that repeats itself in many areas of human thought, and it is no surprise that it should be found in legal history.

In Maine's account this conception among the Romans derived from a pressing practical necessity. The increasing number of foreigners (chiefly traders) on Roman soil created the need for some way of resolving disputes arising among them and between them and Roman citizens. The existing Roman law was quite unsuited to this purpose. Its forms were cumbersome

and interwoven with the idiom of the Latin language. The
search was then for those principles of law that might be said
to be common to all legal systems. Thus it was found that
everywhere title to movable property (chattels or slaves) was
transferred by some ceremony that included a handing over
('manual tradition') of the thing in question. The difference was
that this simple act of transferring possession was, in different
legal systems, accompanied by elaborate ceremonies that obscured an essential unity of form.

In Maine's account, the search for the elements common to
different legal systems was originally regarded simply as an
expedient of commerce, as a means of arriving at some system
of rules suitable for application to persons of diverse origin.
But gradually, and under the influence of Greek philosophy,
there arose the notion that all legal systems were derived from
some original model whose simple and elegant lines had been
obscured by the corruptions of a later age. By stripping off
these corruptions the essential unity of all legal systems, it was
thought, might be revealed. There thus came into being the
myth of a lost code of Nature.

It is not necessary here to subject to critical analysis Maine's
discussion of this conception as it arose among the Romans.
The essential notion is that of a reform of the law actually
projecting itself into the future but presented as recapturing a
former state of excellence.

The affinity between this mode of reform and the legal
fiction is at once apparent. Like the fiction, the notion of re-
storing the law to a former state of perfection was probably
guided by an instinct for continuity and integration. It searched
out in the existing law those elements thought to be basic and
fundamental, the core of excellence, as it were, that had sur-
vived the corruptions of time. Around this core, it built its
reforms, or rather – it would be more appropriate to say –
from this core, it *drew* its reforms. For like the fiction, the
notion of recapturing a lost excellence was a theory of implicit
law. The fiction treated the reform it accomplished as already
latent in the existing law, requiring only a little imagination,
and a talent for bold metaphor, to be brought to realization.

So the theory which took over a later and broader task of reform also thought of itself as bringing forth from the existing law something that was truly there from the beginning.

In the sixth and final phase of Maine's account we reach the stage of *Legislation*. Men finally arrive at a recognition of the simple fact that law can be brought into existence by explicit declarations of intention, incorporated in the words of legal enactments.

The transition to the phase of legislation was not, at least in most societies, as simple as Maine's account makes it appear. We shall return shortly to this final stage in Maine's progression to point out some of the obscurities and uncertainties of function that surrounded the earliest approaches to explicit lawmaking. Meanwhile it will be well, however, to recognize some of the major qualifications that must be projected upon Maine's analysis as a whole.

Certainly Maine's account is mistaken if it means to assert that legal history in all societies has followed exactly the course set by his six stages, or if it assumes that each of these stages is entirely closed out before the next begins. In fact, manifestations of Maine's intermediate stages characteristically spill over, as it were, both backward and forward in time.

Thus, in the Anglo-American countries, though the possibility of an explicit lawmaking power has been recognized for centuries, the fiction still finds occasional employment as a device for extending or modifying existing law. A quite modern instance of its use may be instructive. The body of law in question is that having to do with the obligation of a landowner to keep his premises in a safe condition. In this connection a quite understandable distinction had developed between *trespassers* and *invitees*. The landowner has, it was held, no obligation towards trespassers to keep his property in a safe condition for their unauthorized prowlings. If a trespasser falls into an uncovered hole, he will have to meet his own hospital bill. A different rule had been laid down for those who come on the premises with the express or implied permission of the landowner – for such persons as the guest, the postman, and the delivery boy. If persons in this category – called 'invitees' –

were injured because the landowner had been careless about
the way he kept up his property, then the landowner would
have to respond in damages.

The case then arose of small children coming on the premises
without the permission of the owner, but attracted to the property, let us say, by a seesaw in the backyard. The board of the
seesaw had become rotted and the children are injured as a
result of its collapse under their weight. Is the owner liable?
The children did not come on the premises with the consent of
the owner, and had he known they were there he would no
doubt have asked them to leave. In cases like this, however,
the courts have generally held the owner legally responsible
for the children's injuries. This holding has sometimes been
accomplished by what has been regarded as a fiction. The
children, so it was said, were deemed 'invitees'; the attractive-
ness of the seesaw constituted a kind of invitation foreseeably
drawing them to the owner's property.

Now plainly, the same result could have been reached without fiction. Indeed, a staunch adherent of the Austinian view
that all true law is made law would insist that regardless of the
verbal cover clothing its action, the court was in fact making a
new rule, since the case of trespassing children was in fact not
foreseen by the existing law. Yet the use of the fiction here
proceeds from motives not unlike those that attended its use
in more primitive times. It expresses a desire to treat new law
as being implicit in existing law and as being drawn out of that
law, rather than as being projected upon it as an explicit reform. And who is to say which interpretation is the more ten-
dentious? From a commonsense viewpoint, are not the children
attracted to the premises by a device suited to their playful instincts more like adult invitees than they are like adult trespassers?

If, as the illustration just discussed reveals, the legal fiction
is not yet dead, it is by no means clear that the notion of
explicit legislation was as late in coming to life as Maine's
account suggests. It would seem probable that at least sporadic
instances of explicit lawmaking would occur in quite primitive
societies, perhaps as a response to some special urgency or
confrontation with some new situation quite unlike those to

which the existing law was adjusted. There are, however, two difficulties in determining the extent to which this occurred.

The first lies in deciding what shall count as 'law' and what as the mere exercise of the prerogatives of power. That a primitive ruler might successfully order the execution without trial of a cousin suspected of aspiring to his throne does not mean that he would be equally successful in attempting to change the fundamental rules of his society concerning property, marriage, and inheritance, or, indeed, that it would even occur to him that he could do such a thing. Even today we make a distinction between an executive order and a standing rule of law, and there is every reason to suppose that a similar distinction, with a quite different factual coverage, would exist in more primitive societies.

The second difficulty lies in the fact that in primitive societies any explicit modifications of fundamental law would be likely to be accompanied by claims of supernatural inspiration. The ruler who accomplished such modifications would be likely to treat himself not as a legislator but as a mere conduit through which occult forces expressed themselves. The question then becomes whether we should treat such instances as law made under cover of a disguise or accept a contemporary interpretation which may have been shared by all concerned, including the ruler himself.

These, then, are considerations that warn against an uncritical acceptance of a view of legal history that cuts it up into an invariant sequence of distinct stages. A similar caution, as we have already suggested, applies to any supposition that at the end of the development men drop all coy indirectness in lawmaking and at once embark upon explicit legislation.

In fact our modern legislatures are the remote descendants of assemblies that mixed, in uncertain proportions, law finding with law making. This obscurity of function was often compounded, as it were, by an uncertainty concerning the division of powers among the different agencies of government. A king and his council might, for example, be set over against a popular assembly, with no precise demarcation of functions between them. The resulting rivalry might represent not merely a crude struggle for power but a competition between two regimes of social order: on the one hand, a regime of customary law tempered by intermittent executive decrees; on the other, a regime of statutory law gradually absorbing and re-shaping the pre-existing customary law.

The English Parliament in its origin was primarily an adjudicative or 'law-finding' body, and it only gradually began openly to assert legislative powers. This transition was not without its difficulties. The judgment of a court binds only those who are parties to the litigation before the court or those who derive their rights from the parties. The judgment may, of course, serve as a precedent in a second law suit, but it does not automatically set the rights of anyone not 'privy', as the expression was, to the original judicial determination. But a statute, without more, commonly sets the rights of everyone in the kingdom. How, then, can we rescue a statute of Parliament from the limitations inherent in its judicial power? The answer was found in a fiction: everyone in the kingdom is to be deemed a party to the proceedings of Parliament when it acts as a legislative body.

Unlike most fictions, this one did not pass out of use when it had discharged its original functions, but became a part of traditional legal learning. So in the 18th century we find Blackstone using it to explain why a citizen can be bound by a statute even if it is published in a form not accessible to him, so that he could not posibly know of it:

... every man in England is, in judgment of law, party to the making of an act of parliament, being present thereat by his representatives.

If in Parliament legislative and judicial functions were only gradually separated, so the judiciary itself did not originally consider that it faced statutes in a purely subservient role or that its sole duty was to give effect to the declared intention of Parliament. The judges believed that they, too, were able to draw new law 'out of the old books'. Accordingly, they rather freely extended or curtailed the scope of legislative enactments and sometimes even treated them as inoperative in cases where

Parliament had not, in their opinion, correctly perceived what the situation demanded in the way of law. Thus, the birth of the modern notion of 'made' law was a long and painful process.

The curious reluctance with which men came to accept the notion that law could issue directly from a determinate human source becomes more understandable if we consider for a moment the analogy of religion. The ingredients of religious faith have been found implicit in many aspects of human experience: in the order and harmony revealed by the world around us, in departures from the lawfulness of nature suggesting divine intervention, in the violence of the clouds, in the quiet of the seas, in the whole immensity of the universe, in the goal-seeking qualities of living matter, in the accomplishments of human intelligence. But it would never occur to anyone – except a scoffer viewing the matter from outside – that the tenets of any religious faith could be *enacted* by mere human beings uninspired by sources outside themselves. When we recall the close association between religion and law in primitive society, it becomes understandable why man has been so reluctant to give up the belief that law comes to him from something outside and bigger than himself.

So much, then, by way of an account of the interplay of the notions of made law and implicit law in the course of legal history. We turn now to that interplay as it manifests itself in contemporary society.

Implicit elements in made law

As we have previously remarked, legal philosophy tends to be dominated by a kind of undeclared war between those who believe that all true law is implicit law and those who have a strong preference for what may be called the intellectual flavour of made law. As we have suggested, our object is not to decide which of these predilections is 'right', but rather to render to each view what is justly due to it.

In the present section we shall call the advocates of made law to account for their sins of distortion and omission. In this we shall be continuing the discussion initiated when we analysed the artificialities introduced by Austin's attempt to remake customary law into a special variety of made law.

In the section following this – *Made Elements in Implicit Law* – we shall reverse the tables. In that section we shall attempt to show how the realities of law making and law administering are falsified by any attempt to remake – or, perhaps it should be said, to 'unmake' – all legal phenomena after the image of implicit law.

In the present analysis – concerned with the implicit elements in made law – we shall begin with what is probably the most pervasive of all problems encountered in administering a system of made laws, that of *interpretation*. As we have previously had occasion to remark, the difficulties involved in interpreting statutes are commonly much greater than the layman is inclined to suppose. For the judge, these difficulties are compounded by the circumstance that the easy cases are often settled out of court and hence do not come up for judicial decision.

Let us suppose that in the centre of a large city there is a spacious and attractive park. To protect the park against unwelcome intrusions a statute is enacted making it a misdemeanour to bring any 'vehicle' within the park area. What counts as a 'vehicle' for purposes of this law? There are cases easy to decide: a ten-ton truck is excluded; a perambulator is admitted. It should be noted that these two decisions are not made easy because they can be derived from the dictionary. *Webster's New International* (2nd ed.), for example, defined a vehicle as 'that in or on which a person or thing is or may be carried...' Now plainly by that definition perambulators and trucks are equally apt objects for the epithet 'vehicle'.

Why, then, is it easy to see that a truck is excluded, while a perambulator is admitted? It is not by looking at the word 'vehicle' that we reach this conclusion, but by considering what is implicit in the notion of a park. This is true even though the word 'park' nowhere appears in the statute; its language may speak not of 'the city park', but of 'all that area bounded on the north by Adams Boulevard, on the east by Third Street', etc. What we are basically interpreting, then, is not a word, but an institution and its meaning for the lives of the human beings affected by it.

It follows that the proper interpretation of the ordinance will depend on the meaning attributed to the institution 'park' by the practices and attitudes of the society in question. In some countries – in the cooler latitudes, for example – a park tends to be a place of quiet and repose, where the citizen may escape the tumult of the city. In the warmer latitudes it may be a place of music and gaiety, to which the citizen will betake himself after his need for repose has been satisfied by a siesta. Now this difference in the meaning of the institution may have an important bearing on the interpretation of the word 'vehicle'. A steam calliope may be welcomed to one kind of park, for example, as a contribution to its merriment; indeed, an ingenious police sergeant might justify a ruling that it may come in by reasoning that the calliope is not really a 'vehicle' at all, since it carries nothing but itself, being a musical instrument mounted on wheels. By the same token a hearse – with its sinister burden – would be definitely excluded. In another clime, where parks mean something quite different, these rulings might be reversed.

Now at this point a strong adherent of the view that all true law is made law would be likely to enter an objection along these lines: Of course, when a legislator uses language he intends that language to have the meaning it has in his culture; he is himself a participant in that culture and he means by his words not what the dictionary says they mean, but what his fellow citizens would mean when they use them. Thus the local significance of the institution 'park' naturally enters into the meaning of the statute which his lawmaking brings into existence. That the linguistic ingredients of which the statute is fabricated are in part, as it were, locally grown does not mean that the statute is any the less made law.

But this is too simple – and too static – a view of the matter. In the first place, as we have already pointed out, the word 'park' may not appear in the statute at all. Furthermore, insofar as the lawmaker had any clearly definable intention, it may have been directed to objects, such as the ten-ton truck, that would be excluded by any reasonable conception to a park anywhere. The troublesome cases are in reality resolved not in advance by the legislator, but at the point of application. This means that in applying the statute the judge or police sergeant must be guided not simply by its words but also by some conception of what is fit and proper to come into a park; conceptions of this sort are implicit in the practices and attitudes of the society of which he is a member. Finally, the social institution 'park' and the legal regulations relevant to it may be expected with the passage of time to influence one another reciprocally. A lax administration of the law excluding 'vehicles' may gradually change the cultural meaning of 'park'. Conversely, a wholly extra-legal change in the uses made of parks may gradually bring about an alteration in the meaning of the statute. All this adds up to the conclusion that an important part of the statute in question is not made by the legislator, but grows and develops as an implication of complex practices and attitudes which may themselves be in a state of development and change.

In any modern legal system, illustrations like that of the park and the vehicles could be multiplied many times over. There are, indeed, few statutes that may properly be called self-applying, that require for their interpretation merely a familiarity with the ordinary meaning of words. A statute requiring vehicles to pass on the right may seem to have a geometric simplicity about it that dispenses with the need for any thought process not already pursued by the legislator. But if the statute means that the driver must pass the *oncoming* vehicle on the right, it may be viewed as containing an implication (derived from the necessities of orderly traffic) that a driver *overtaking* another vehicle should normally pass it on the left – an implication of his lawmaking that the original legislator may or may not have perceived himself.

The interpretation of statutes is, then, not simply a process of drawing out of the statute what its maker put into it but is also in part, and in varying degrees, a process of adjusting the statute to the implicit demands and values of the society to which it is to be applied. In this sense it may be said that no enacted law ever comes from its legislator wholly and fully 'made'.

When a court is confronted with *contradictory* statutes emanating from the same lawmaker it becomes impossible to pretend that the judge merely draws from the words of the law what the legislator put into them, for in this case what the lawmaker has put into them is an unmanageable jumble of meaning. To make sense of statutes that contradict one another the judge must of necessity take his guidance from some principle not expressed in the statute themselves. One of the most perceptive discussions of this problem is one written in 1788 by Alexander Hamilton:

It not uncommonly happens that there are two statutes existing at one time, clashing in whole or in part with each other, and neither of them containing any repealing clause or expression. In such a case it is the province of the courts to liquidate and fix their meaning and operation. So far as they can, by any fair construction, be reconciled to each other, reason and law conspire to dictate that this should be done; where this is impracticable, it becomes a matter of necessity to give effect to one in exclusion of the other. The rule which has obtained in the courts for determining their relative validity is, that the last in order of time shall be preferred to the first. But this is a mere rule of construction, not derived from any positive law, but from the nature and reason of the thing. It is a rule not enjoined upon the courts by legislative provision, but adopted by themselves, as consonant to truth and propriety, for the direction of their conduct as interpreters of the law. They thought it reasonable that between the interfering acts of an *equal* authority, that which was the last indication of its will should have the preference. (*The Federalist*, No. 78.)

Now it can safely be said that there is implicit in the very notion of a progressive society a general assumption that later laws should control earlier enactments. This seems to modern man the most obvious common sense. But we must remember that over most of the world's history the notion of a kind of natural law of human progress was alien to men's thinking. In a society dominated by a belief that man had fallen from a former state of perfection there would be every reason for reversing the preference between earlier and later laws. There are indeed in the old law books statements to the effect that between two contradictory royal charters, the prior in time prevails. The matter would not be easy to bring to an explicit test, however, for the simple reason that during most of human history the very notion of a *made* law was unknown. It is only the made law, it should be remembered, that carries with it any clear indication of the date of its inception. Where all laws are thought of as being, in principle, timeless, the problem of the conflict of laws through time can scarcely present itself as a distinct issue. In such an intellectual climate the question would be, not which law undoes the other, but which is and always was the true law.

In analyzing implicit elements in made law we have so far identified those elements as they affect the interpretation of statutes and the reconciliation of statutes when they are inconsistent with one another. The problem runs deeper, however, and touches the very meaning of law itself. Every exercise of the lawmaking function is accompanied by certain tacit assumptions, or implicit expectations, about the kind of product that will emerge from the legislator's efforts and the form he will give to that product. A somewhat bizarre illustration may serve to make this point clear. Suppose that in a newly created nation a written constitution has been adopted after lengthy consideration. This constitution has been drafted with great care and every precaution has been taken to state clearly *who* can make law and by what *rules* the lawmaking authority must proceed if it is to make laws that will bind the citizen. The new constitution, we shall suppose, provides that the supreme lawmaking power shall be vested in a legislature, the members of which are to be selected by balloting procedures clearly set forth in the constitution itself. All of these rules are followed faithfully. When the new legislature meets, its first act is to pass a resolution that all laws enacted by it shall be kept secret from the citizenry. There is in this act no violation of the language of the constitution, for it says nothing whatever about the publication of laws, being in this respect like the Constitution of the United States.

Surely, it will be said, there is implicit in the very notion of a law the assumption that its contents will, in some manner or other, be made accessible to the citizen so that he will have some chance to know what it says and be able to obey it. But to say this is to assert, in effect, that the lawmaking process is itself subject to implicit laws. This is obviously not an assumption that will appeal to those who insist that all true law is made law. Nor does the difficulty end with unpublished laws. What shall we say of the wholly unintelligible law? The statute with an internal contradiction such that it appears to nullify itself? The law that purports to impose a duty to perform some act that lies beyond human capacities? The retrospective law declaring illegal an act that was perfectly lawful when performed?

It may be said that the possibility of such legislative aberrations is ruled out by common sense and ordinary conceptions of decency. History, however, offers little support for this assurance. Retrospective criminal statutes, for example, have made their appearance down through the centuries and in a great variety of human contexts. To be sure, if your object in making law is to lay down rules by which people may guide their conduct, then your laws will operate prospectively and will govern only those actions which take place after their enactment. But if you possess the lawmaking power, and you wish to get rid of an enemy who has violated no law in the books, what expedient is more apt to occur to you than to enact a 'law' declaring what he did last week to be a capital offence?

Abuses of this sort reached a grotesque climax during the Nazi regime in Germany. The ordinary expectations that accompany lawmaking were violated by Hitler's government on an unprecedented scale. Special military courts trying citizens accused of subversive acts often reached convictions in complete disregard of the provisions enacted by the Nazis themselves for the decision of such cases, thus making it pointless for the German citizen to study the Nazi statutes to see what he could and could not do under the new regime. Retrospective legislation was freely employed. It is said that many 'secret laws' were passed, though it is not easy to know to what extent this occurred, for the Nazis were extremely casual about giving any publicity to their 'laws'. There are scholars who have insisted that, though the statutes enacted under Hitler were thoroughly evil in their objectives, they were nevertheless just as much laws as were those enacted in England or Switzerland. In terms of the analysis presented here, such a view implies that the lawmaking power, once accepted as such, can contain no implicit limitations – there are no implicit laws of lawmaking. If this view were consistently maintained it would mean that a whole book of laws enacted secretly and locked in a vault would be 'just as much law' as a compilation of rules put in the hands of every citizen and expressed in the plainest vernacular of the people to whom it was applicable.

In many countries there are, of course, written constitutions which regulate and control the making of laws. Such a constitution may prescribe the form a statute must take in order to be valid; in other words, the constitution may lay down in advance rules for determining what kinds of legislative acts shall count as laws. Where such a constitution exists, it may seem there would be no occasion for the courts to resort to any implicit understanding about the nature of law – a kind of man-made 'higher law' fully capable of answering the question whether a given legislative act is entitled to be called a law.

But there are at least four reasons why failure must attend any such attempt to rescue made law from dependence on implicit or inherent 'laws of lawmaking'. *First*, the most grotesque aberrations from ordinary conceptions of what law means are precisely those which the constitutional draftsman is most likely to leave out of account. One of the most obvious things about a law is that there ought to be some way for the citizen to find out what it says, yet the Constitution of the United States contains no provision requiring the publication of laws. The explanation for this kind of omission is suggested in the following passage from the philosopher Wittgenstein:

Someone says to me: 'Shew the children a game.' I teach them gaming with dice, and the other says, 'I didn't mean that sort of game.' Must the exclusion of the game with dice have come before his mind when he gave me the order?

Certainly the one who gave the order would be entitled to reply: 'Obviously I did not mean to include gambling with dice, and the proof of this is not that I consciously excluded it, but that such a "game" did not even remotely enter my mind as a possibility; in my conscious calculations there was simply no occasion to direct my mind toward such a bizarre outcome.'

Had there been a written constitution in Imperial Rome it is certainly doubtful whether the draftsmen could have anticipated that the Emperor Caligula would appoint his horse as consul or that he would circumvent a requirement that laws be publicly posted by putting his own in such fine print and hanging them so high that no one could read them.

The writing of constitutions becomes impossible unless the draftsman can assume that the legislator shares with him some implicit notions of the limits of legal decency and sanity. If the draftsman were to attempt to forestall in advance every conceivable aberration of the legislative power, his constitution would resemble a museum of freaks and monsters. It is certainly difficult to imagine such a constitution serving an educational function or offering a suitable object for a pledge of allegiance.

There is another, and in our sequence, *second*, reason why a written constitution cannot successfully control legislation entirely by principles that have themselves been previously legislated. This lies in the fact that a purported statute that seems in one context inconsistent with the very idea of law, in another context may serve the cause of legal decency. The retrospective statute is a good example.

If a law is to guide the conduct of the citizen subject to it, then it seems obvious that it must operate *prospectively*, that it must tell the citizen what he should do *after* its enactment and not what he should have done before it went into effect. To this sober common sense the draftsmen of the Constitution of New Hampshire added a note of moral indignation when they inserted in their charter of lawmaking (1784) the following language:

Retrospective laws are highly injurious, oppressive. and unjust.

No such laws, therefore, should be made, either for the decision of civil causes, or the punishment of offenses.

This would seem to take care of the matter and to convert into an explicit, made rule what was previously only implicit in ordinary ways of thinking about law. But trouble lay ahead for the courts charged with applying this provision. What shall we say of a situation like this: A legislature enacts a law providing that henceforth no marriage shall be valid unless the person performing the ceremony fills out a form provided by the state and returns it to a central bureau within five days of the ceremony. Shortly before the statute goes into effect, a fire destroys the state printing office, and for six months it is impossible for the state to provide the required forms. Meanwhile the legislature has adjourned and there is no lawful way of repealing the statute or postponing its effective date. Before the legislature can meet again hundreds of couples go through the marriage ceremony, and since the required forms could not be filled, their marriages are, by the relevant statute, legally invalid and any children born of their union illegitimate. When the legislature meets again its first act is to pass a statute retrospectively curing the defect in the marriages that have meanwhile taken place.

The New Hampshire Supreme Court was in fact confronted with the necessity of passing on the constitutional validity of curative measures of this sort, though to be sure in a somewhat less dramatic context than that just supposed. They faced the embarrassment of having to decide that the Constitutional provision did not, despite its categorical language, really mean what it said and that some kinds of retrospective legislation were not only not 'highly injurious, oppressive, and unjust' but were innocent and beneficial.

This experience might suggest converting the perceived implicit necessity for retrospective legislation in certain situations into an explicit, made rule of constitutional law. Why not, for example, amend the provision against retrospective laws by adding the words: '... but this provision shall not apply to laws intended to cure defects of legal form'?

But this would never do. Suppose a citizen accused of murder is tried, convicted, and sentenced to be hanged at a trial presided over by a man who appeared to hold the office of judge, but who, as the result of some 'irregularity', did not lawfully hold that position. Surely before considering a law that would retrospectively validate the purported judge's authority we would want to know more about the 'irregularity' affecting his position. And to be reminded of the monstrous things that can be done in the name of curative legislation we need only make another short visit to that chamber of legal horrors, Hitler's Germany. In 1934 trouble was brewing in the Nazi party, the dissident elements apparently grouping themselves about Ernst Röhm in Munich. When Hitler got wind of this development, he and his followers made a hasty trip to Munich where they shot down Röhm and some seventy of his supporters. On his return to Berlin Hitler declared that in taking this measure he had acted as 'the supreme judicial power of the German people'. The fact that he had not lawfully been appointed to any such office, and that no trial had ever been held of the condemned men – these 'irregularities of form' were promptly rectified by a statute retrospectively converting the shootings into lawful executions.

The example of retrospective laws illustrates how difficult it is to convert the implicit demands of legal decency into explicit constitutional limitations. It will be useful to consider briefly another example of this difficulty. It is ancient wisdom, tracing back at least as far as the Roman taboo against the *privilegium*, that laws ought to be *general*, they ought to be addressed, not to particular persons, but to persons generally or to classes of persons (say, 'all householders'). Accordingly, a number of American states have inserted in their constitutions prohibitions against 'private or special' statutes. These have given rise to endless difficulties.

The trouble is that the private or one-man statute, like the retrospective statute, can only be judged in its specific context. We have already* given an example of an innocent and beneficial 'private law', a *privilegium* that served, rather than disserved, the cause of legality. A bribed judge improperly holds

* See pp. 24–6.

a patent invalid. Seven years go by before his perfidy is discovered; the case is reheard by a reconstituted court, which declares the patent valid. This gives the injured party back his patent, but does nothing about the seven years during which he was deprived of the profits he would otherwise have obtained from it. This is an injustice the courts are powerless to correct; they have no authority to grant or extend patents; the issuing of patents rests with the Patent Office acting under an act of Congress. The cure for the situation was found in a special act of Congress extending the life of the patent for seven years. No constitutional difficulty arose, for it happens that the Constitution of the United States contains no general provision against special or private legislation, an omission which has historically, in turn, facilitated abuses that would not be possible under many state constitutions.

It will be well to recall that we are now discussing the extent to which a written constitution can dispense with the necessity for resorting to what may be called 'implicit laws of lawmaking' or limitations on governmental power resting in generally received conceptions of what is meant by a regime of order founded on law. We have pointed out, first, that it is impossible (and would probably be undesirable) for the constitutional draftsman to attempt to forestall all the more bizarre ways in which the expectations that normally accompany exercises of governmental power may be violated; a provision requiring that the consulship be held by a human being, and not a horse, would make strange reading in any constitution. We have further observed, secondly, that certain departures from the usual practices of lawmaking, such as those involved in retrospective and special or one-man statutes, though thoroughly objectionable to most contexts, may in some cases actually serve the ends of legality and fairness.

A *third* limitation on constitutional foresight lies in the difficulty of anticipating possible situations of emergency and of foreseeing what modifications in normal practices may be required in meeting them. One of the most obvious things about a law is that it ought to be published and made available to those subject to it. A natural way of meeting this desideratum in a written constitution is to prescribe some form of publication, with a stipulation that no statute shall go into effect until, say, one week after its first publication, thus allowing time for the word to get around, as it were. This delay, beneficial under normal circumstances, may become disastrous under the conditions of a sudden national emergency. At the same time, under such conditions it may be pointless to delay the statute's effective date; with everyone watching and listening to learn what the legislature will do, news of the enactment is likely to spread very rapidly.

As is well known, some constitutions have granted to the government a power to declare the existence of a state of national emergency; during this officially declared emergency certain constitutional restraints on governmental power are suspended. The experience with such provisions has not been a happy one. Paradoxically, it may conceivably be better to rest departures from constitutional restraints on an implicit necessity, readily perceived by the overwhelming majority of citizens, rather than on an explicit grant of authority which may serve to give despotism words on paper to point to as proof of its legality.

There is a *fourth* and final reason why a written constitution cannot dispense with the need for a resort to implicit or unwritten principles of legal decency and orderly government. This lies in the simple fact that before they can be applied, the words of a constitution require to be interpreted. In our discussion so far we have been assuming that the vital task of interpretation will be taken over by the regular courts of law, as it has been in the United States. There are nations, however, with written constitutions whose interpretation is entrusted to special 'constitutional courts' or is even left with the legislature itself, which is thus assigned the task of interpreting the limits of its own power. For our present purposes it is enough to observe that, whatever the agency charged with the task of interpretation, that task – when approached conscientiously – remains much the same and presents essentially the same problems.

We have previously pointed out* how fallacious it is to suppose that in interpreting a statute the judge simply draws out of its text a meaning that the legislature has put there. In the case of a hypothetical statute prohibiting vehicles from entering a park we noted that in determining the effect of the statute the court would have to ask itself: What are parks for anyway? The answer to this question must largely be drawn from what may be called implicit sources, from the attitudes and practices of the community, and some shared conception of the most beneficial use of park areas. The considerations that make it vain to suppose that a statute can be cut loose from the developing life into which it is projected apply with a vengeance to the interpretation of constitutions.

In the United States the best illustration of this touches the central feature of the whole constitutional system, namely, the power of the courts to declare statutes unconstitutional. This all-important power is nowhere explicitly conferred on the judiciary by the words of the Constitution. At best it can be seen as an oblique implication of words primarily addressed to other subjects. The most secure foundation for the power does not, however, rest on the text of the Constitution, but lies rather in a necessity implicit in the whole frame of government brought into existence by the Constitution. This last consideration is most persuasive in those cases where, the laws of the federal Congress and those of a state legislature being in conflict, the court determines the jurisdictional boundaries that separate state and federal powers. Without this particular judicial power it is difficult to see how the American federal system could have functioned at all. The power had to be and therefore was.

Any modern governmental structure involves a complex system of interrelated and complementary powers. By some means or other these powers must be kept in jibe with one another. The obvious and tempting way to accomplish this is to bring them all under a central despotic power. This solution would mean, of course, the end of constitutionalism. On the other hand, no constitutional draftsman can foresee what

* See pp. 83–5.

points of rub and friction will develop in the future as the structure he has created feels the strain of new and novel demands. The solution must be found in an interpretation of the constitution that will respect not merely its words but the implicit ideals of orderly and decent government those words attempted to express.

Reflecting on the complexity of modern constitutions and their tragic dependence on the integrity, judgement, and insight of those who must interpret and administer them, one may almost be inclined to yearn for the simpler days of the absolute monarch. In those days what the ruler said *was* law and that was an end of it. Then was the heyday of made law, when human fiat could bring law into existence pure and undefiled by any contamination of 'laws of lawmaking', whether written or unwritten. Or so it may seem from our perspective. The reality was much more complex.

We have already pointed out that Maine's last stage in the evolution of law, that of legislation, by no means came into existence overnight. The first ventures into this field were tentative and fragmentary. The 'absolute' monarch might be able to order a commoner to give up his wife to him, but it did not follow that he would be able, or that he would suppose he would be able, to command a fundamental revision in the general laws of marriage. Furthermore, if he felt any inclination toward broad legislation of this sort, there would be learned men and priests about him ready to tell him what he might do and not do 'lawfully' in the way of lawmaking.

The most important 'unmade' limitation on the monarch's lawmaking lies, however, in the fact that his reign must sooner or later come to an end. If he is lucky enough to hold the throne until his death, there must be some way of designating his successor. The principle most consonant with the theory that all true law is made law would be, of course, a rule by which the lawmaker himself had the power to name his successor. In the course of history a rule of this sort has from time to time emerged, but it has never achieved secure acceptance, since men in their full powers do not like rivals, even of their own choice, and men whose powers are waning seldom make good kingmakers, even assuming, as is improbable, that they will recognize that the time has come to designate a successor.

In actual practice, succession is commonly made to depend on some defined relationship to the departing monarch. If the relationship is simple (say, that of being the eldest son) the rule may default because the designated successor does not exist or is incompetent. If the rule is complex, covering a wide range of relationships, it can easily give rise to disputes and civil war. But, whatever the rule of succession may be, it can never be simply a *made* or enacted rule. It must rest on a perceived need for some institutional backstop against chaos, and its terms will normally be found not in enactment, but in a received tradition reinforced by a general conviction of its essential rightness.

The monarchical principle of lawmaking suffers its most serious crisis when the monarch is displaced before his death. This displacement, or the threat of it, may come about in a variety of ways. A self-appointed council of elder statesmen, acting perhaps without the support of precedent, declares the monarch incompetent; a rival to the throne discloses an apparent flaw in the title of the occupant and claims the throne for himself; a rebellious faction seeks by armed force to oust the reigning sovereign. Historians are likely to construe such events in terms of a sheer struggle for power. But these struggles are seldom unaccompanied by claims of rightfulness; both sides will normally make some pretence to the support of implicit law. There is usually much that is specious in these claims. But the fact that such claims are made, and that action is taken in the name of them, tends, when the dust has settled, to restrain the victorious party. Having achieved its position in the name of law, it has taken on itself an obligation towards the principles of legal morality; it has, in effect, entered a tacit agreement with its subjects to make its laws with due regard to what we have here termed 'the implicit laws of lawmaking'.

One final problem deserves brief consideration before we quit the subject of implicit elements in made law. This is the problem presented by a situation like the following. An established government is overthrown by violence; the rebellious party holds power for six months, during which time it repeals many laws of the old regime and enacts new ones in their stead; the old regime then returns to power. What laws now govern events that occurred during the six months while the rebels held the reins of government? Do we make bastards of all the children of marriages contracted under new marriage laws enacted by the intervening regime and now repealed by the returning government? If we declare these marriages legally valid, do we also uphold every confiscation of property accomplished under laws enacted by the now deposed regime?

These are perplexing problems, and they have arisen historically in a great variety of contexts. The predicament of postwar Germany in liquidating the abuses of law that occurred under Hitler serves to remind us of how agonizing these problems can be. On the other hand, the German experience may easily mislead us into thinking that it is only some monstrous distortion of ordinary moral values that can give rise to such problems. This is far from being the case.

Toward the end of World War II, as the German troops were being driven out of France, a vacuum of governmental power was left behind that had to be filled in some manner. Impromptu governments were put together by the French people. Men volunteered themselves for the office of mayor or judge, much as during some emergency an ordinary citizen might on his own initiative take over the role of traffic officer. Improvised courts were set up for trying persons charged with improper collaboration with the occupying troops. Most of what happened during this period was probably well intentioned, though of course abusive exercises of power were bound to occur. When a more orderly government was established, it faced the task of sifting through the legal debris left behind, confirming this act despite its irregularity, nullifying that act despite, perhaps, its outward respect for legal form.

During the 1840s the state of Rhode Island underwent a somewhat similar experience. In a little-remembered civil war known as Dorr's Rebellion, that tiny commonwealth for a time enjoyed the doubtful blessing of having two rival governments, each with its own written constitution and both voted into power, though at different times and by differently qualified electorates. When the dispute was finally resolved, the legal entanglements left behind were like those that follow any period during which it is not possible to say clearly who has the authority to make law and who has not. The fact that in Rhode Island little blood was shed, and that no really deep-dyed villains appeared on either side, hardly made those problems simpler.

Reflection on historical incidents like these, falling as they do outside the ordinary range of human experience, can impart important lessons about law. There are at least three: (1) Normal processes for making law can fail, or fall into confusion, from a variety of causes; human perfidy is only one of these. (2) In leading a society back to a condition where legality is a realizable ideal, no guidance can be obtained from a philosophy which asserts that the only true law is made law; this philosophy is a luxury to be enjoyed after the return trip is over. (3) The legal measures necessary to accomplish this return will of necessity include some that would be thoroughly reprehensible under normal conditions. The most indispensable of these measures is the retrospective statute, condemned by the New Hampshire constitution as 'injurious, oppressive, and unjust'. To paraphrase Walter Bagehot, we may say that the bottom steps of the ladder leading back to legality are very steep.

Made elements in implicit law

In the section just concluded we have attempted to show why no edifice of made law can rest entirely on itself. We have sought to demonstrate how any such system must find its anchorage in supports that are not themselves brought into existence by enactment, but derive instead from a perceived implicit need.

It is now time to reverse the direction of our inquiry. Up to now we have been attempting to identify the generally unnoticed implicit elements in systems of made law. We now turn to the opposite task of identifying elements of made law that inconspicuously help to shape systems of rules that are thought to be entirely implicit. Our chief interest will be in a subject that served to initiate the discussion in our last section, namely, customary law.

We have already discussed at some length* John Austin's attempt to remake customary law into something more congenial to his system, a system founded on the premise that all true law is law made or enacted by public authority. If this attempt of Austin's misses its mark, the same cannot be said of his wry characterization of a certain attitude towards customary law. He remarks that the 'admirers of customary law love to trick out their idol with mysterious and imposing attributes'.

This understates the case. In the literature of legal philosophy there appears from time to time a veritable *mystique* of customary law. Let us present this conception in its most romantic and unbuttoned form: The finest intellectual and moral qualities of man are expressed in customary law. This law is not imposed by a ruler on a subject, but arises spontaneously out of the dealings of one man with another. The sanction behind this law is not brute force, but a perceived need, a need discerned intuitively by those most directly affected by it. Customary law is infinitely superior to law made by parliamentary procedures, where the issues are distorted by specious rationalizations, and the final enactment mutilated by last-minute compromises, often accomplished by political leaders who do not really understand the problems involved. Customary law is also vastly superior to that laid down in judicial decisions, rendered by judges remote from life, argued over in an atmosphere of abstraction, and fitted finally into a Procrustean bed of precedent. Customary law is not only better in substance than legislated or adjudicated law, but is also more truly democratic in its origin than any other form of law. It is a law brought into existence not by men making marks opposite printed words on paper ballots, but by men

* See pp. 65–8.

directly guiding their actions towards one another in a way that each perceives to be right and just.

In attempting to present here a somewhat more sober and realistic analysis of customary law, it will be well to begin by drawing into comparison a related form of social order, that presented by explicit contract or agreement. The rules of custom and contract share the quality that both may be said to arise out of the situation of the parties subject to them, instead of being projected upon that situation by some outside authority. We may say that in contract law the 'made' element predominates, while the rules of customary law are commonly thought of as exemplifying 'implicit' law. This combination of affinity and diversity suggests that a comparison of contract and customary law will be useful.

In undertaking that comparison we may begin by observing that, just as appraisals of customary law often run toward poetic extravagance, so a certain mystique often surrounds contract. This social expedient is sometimes depicted as if it offered an assured route to universal peace, as if by resorting to it men of good will could with confidence, and under all circumstances, negotiate away their differences. When deep-cutting disputes arise within a society those responsible for settling them often debate a choice among three possible procedures of solution: 1) a resort to some form of adjudication by an impartial arbiter; 2) a legislative decision; and 3) an urging of the disputants towards some contractual settlement of their differences. At such times one will hear it said, on behalf of the third route, 'A negotiated settlement is *always* better than an imposed one.' Sometimes this assertion seems to carry the implication that such a settlement will not only serve the interests of both parties better than any other but will also bring about a solution that is the best possible from the standpoint of the public interest. This kind of appraisal, by overstating its merits and capacities, does disservice to a useful, and indeed, indispensable form of social ordering.

In moving toward a closer look at contract the first thing to observe is a peculiarity of nomenclature. A contract between two parties, in proper form and for a legitimate object, constitutes, as it were, a miniature statute. If we want to know what the legal rights and duties of the parties are within the area covered by the contract, we look to the terms of the contract itself. In case of dispute the courts interpret and apply those terms much as they would the enactment of a legislature. In spite of this, lawyers do not commonly speak of 'the law of the contract', though the Romans had no scruples about using expressions equivalent to this and the French Civil Code states that a contract has 'the force of law between the parties'.

If we were undeterred by linguistic usage and looked only to substance, the terms of a contract would indeed appear as a special kind of made law. This way of viewing the matter would, however, entail certain inconveniences for any theory which insists that the making of law is a state monopoly and that anything coming from a different source cannot be the genuine product. For if there were such a thing as 'the law of the contract', there would be two kinds of made law: legislated law and contractually created law. The usual solution for this difficulty is to say that the power of contracting parties to create rules binding themselves exists by delegation from, and at the tolerance of, the lawmaking power of the state. This explanation, in turn, encounters the embarrassment that in many countries it is quite impossible to point to any legislative enactment by which private citizens were ever granted the power to bind themselves contractually. This power has for centuries simply been taken for granted; its historical origin has been as a form of implicit law. Generally, then, we may say that if we look not to words but to the realities of social organization: 1) the *terms* of a binding contract constitute a kind of *made law*; 2) the rule or pronciple according to which those terms are regarded as being legally binding is a variety of *implicit law* – if you will, a form of *implicit constitutional law*. In what follows we shall, in any event, disregard the usage of jurists, and speak freely of 'the law of the contract' as a way of saying that the rules established by a contract are binding on the parties and serve to set their legal rights and duties towards each other.

In analysing the contract as a form of social ordering we must begin by setting to one side simple contracts of sale on an open market, in which the only term is that setting the price, such agreements as that by which, for example, A sells one hundred bushels of grain to B at the going market price. The 'law' of such a contract, that is, the price term, results from the state of supply and demand; it is not really *made* by the parties, but is largely *implicit* in a balance of market forces. A contract which significantly serves to create legal rules is one that reaches into the future and sets the terms of a contemplated collaboration between the parties. A is negotiating with B, let us say, an agreement whereby A will serve as agent to sell some product manufactured by B. Under discussion are such questions as: What shall be the duration of the contract – one year, two years, or perhaps five? Shall A be compensated on a straight commission basis, or shall he be guaranteed a certain annual return? Shall provision be made for arbitration in case of dispute, and if so, what procedure shall be set up for selecting the arbitrator?

Now, of course, the influence of market forces will not be without effect on the negotiation of such an agreement. The rate of commission, for example, may be largely removed from the negotiations by a combination of market conditions and standard practice. But there will be a large fringe of indeterminacy affecting the outcome. The final shape of the agreement will be determined by factors like the following: Who is best at wheedling? Who can out-stare the other and shame him into surrender by branding his demands as petty and prompted by an unworthy distrust? Which party is willing to press farthest the game of brinkmanship and thus reap for himself, perhaps, a reward for his own recklessness? Who has at his command the text of similar contracts between other parties, which he can exploit as models for a solution he desires? What alternative opportunities are open to the parties, so that if one of them finds the negotiations going to his disadvantage he can turn elsewhere or threaten to turn elsewhere? Will one of the parties be able to exploit the familiar 'wicked partner' technique, declaring that although the other party's proposal seems

eminently reasonable to him, his partner (who unfortunately
cannot be present) is dead set against it? Is there by good
fortune a friendly intermediary available who can guide the
parties towards, not the one right solution, for there is no such
thing, but towards a reasonable and workable accommodation
of their interests? Are the services of such an intermediary rendered superfluous by the fact that the parties themselves have
a sufficient experience in negotiation, and a sufficient perception
of the routes to a shared success in it, so that each is able to obtain what his interest demands without taking an undue
advantage of the other or building up resentments for the
future?

It is in some such atmosphere, compounded of foresight and
accident, reason and folly, generosity and avarice, that the law
of the contract is brought into existence. What shall we say
of the conditions attending the birth of customary law? At this
point our inquiry becomes more difficult. If we were to attempt
here a thorough-going analysis of customary rules generally,
our discussion would have to include food taboos, the affinity
of customary practices with animistic views of nature, and the
interrelations of custom with the technology of the relevant
society. Any such exploration would lead us far afield. We shall
accordingly concentrate our attention on those rules of customary law that serve directly to regulate, and set limits to,
man's purposively directed interactions with one another.

Within this area of inquiry the first thing to note is that rules
of customary law or, more generally, conceptions that particular kinds of conduct are in certain situations obligatory do not
arise simply out of habitual or repeated actions. The fact that
a man or a group of men has for a long time acted uniformly
in certain respects cannot of itself give anyone else a claim
that this pattern of behaviour should be continued. A sudden
departure from established routine may cause surprise, but it
will not normally arouse a sense of injury or wrong unless the
observer has in some way adjusted his own affairs to the previously observed pattern of behaviour. Customary law imposing rights and duties will arise between A and B only in case
their interests are interwoven in such a way that each has to

orient his own behaviour by some expectation as to the other's actions. If, for example, A and B occupy separate apartments in the same building and share a common entryway, then a practice might grow up whereby A was expected to lock the entry door at night, while it was anticipated that B would unlock it in the morning to let the milkman in. Conceivably such a practice might arise without any words being spoken and yet it might come to represent for both sides a settled division of labour on which each was entitled to rely in guiding his own actions. It would then become for those affected by it something like a miniature system of customary law.

Customary law arises, then, out of situations of human interaction where each participant guides himself by an anticipation of what the other will do and will expect him to do. There is, therefore, in customary law something approaching a contractual element; its underlying principle is a reciprocity of expectations. This is true, in an attenuated fashion, even when a particular custom seems wholly one-sided, as where a tribesman is expected each year at harvest time to render to his chieftain a tribute of five measures of grain. The tribesman guides his conduct by the expectation that the chieftain will not demand more or less; if in fact his demands vary capriciously from year to year, we are dealing not with a customary tribute, but an unregulated exploitation of power, something that is, incidentally, exceedingly rare in primitive society. Indeed even one-sided, but fixed, tributes of the sort just supposed are uncommon in primitive society. Normally the pattern of interaction involves a much richer reciprocity, the chieftain being expected, for example, after he has collected his tributes, to hold a feast (the 'potlatch') for his tribesmen.

The element of reciprocity in customary law becomes increasingly explicit when we move into the area of commercial transactions, where A and B are entering into business relations with one another against a background of established practices and expectations rooted in past dealings between them and other businessmen engaged in similar transactions. In such cases, in judging disputes between A and B, the courts often have the choice of saying that their relations were governed by customary law or of saying that the parties tacitly incorporated into their transactions a commitment to render what was due under standard practice. Often there is little difference between the two explanations. And indeed in our illustration of the two tenants who shared the task of locking and unlocking the door, it would be possible to argue without absurdity that they had tacitly entered a contract for rendering these reciprocal services for one another.

Our treatment of customary law would be seriously distorted if we conveyed the impression that its rules serve always to set the terms of a collaboration between friendly parties. On the contrary, customary law has perhaps performed its most significant historical function in setting limits to conflict between enemies. If it has not succeeded in eliminating warfare, it has at least served to lift it above a blind, reciprocal destructiveness and has instead made of it a purposeful enterprise of restricted goals.

This service of customary law may be illustrated by a practice that once actually existed, though our account of its origin must of necessity rest in large measure on conjecture. Let us suppose that in a primitive society a smouldering hostility has developed between two tribes; a series of irregular and half-hearted skirmishes have taken place between them. Tribe A decides that it is time to bring the matter to an issue. It dispatches a messenger with instructions to cast a spear into the camp of Tribe B. The messenger is provided with a weapon of a type used only by Tribe A, so there will be no doubt of its origin. The messenger is told to throw the spear conspicuously, but so that it will injure no one, and then to retire at once. We are to suppose that this is the first time in history that this device has been employed. The elders of Tribe B decide that they understand the meaning intended to be conveyed; they dispatch a mission to Tribe A and, after some negotiations, a peaceful settlement of differences is arranged. Word of this incident gets about among other tribes, and in the course of time the practice of throwing a spear into the other's camp becomes the accepted way of conveying an ultimatum, so much so that any tribe which opens full-scale hostilities without first employing this ceremony will be condemned for a violation of intertribal law.

From its very first use it is plain that the casting of the spear was intended as a form of communication. What it communicated was somewhat open-ended. It said something like this: 'We demand urgently that you let us know at once your intentions toward us.' The response might, of course, take various forms: an immediate attack (for which, of course, the challenger would be prepared), a counterproposal for discussions, or perhaps the dispatch of a messenger carrying the information that the powerful Tribe X had just joined forces with the challenged tribe, so that the challenger would find it wise to abandon his belligerent intentions.

Whatever the response may turn out to be, there will be involved an expression of reciprocal intentions that we may call an *open-ended kind of bargaining*. Even if the challenged party gives no verbal response, but immediately mounts an attack, this act of violence will have a clarity of meaning that would be lacking if it were not in response to the casting of the spear. Without that background of communication, the attack – in its first phases at least – might be interpreted as a mere continuation of the sporadic skirmishes that had taken place in the past. As it is, the challenger knows at once what his opposite number has in mind and can shape his own actions accordingly.

The suggestion that customary law originates in an 'open-ended kind of bargaining' may be extended to customary practices generally, including those that regulate dealings between friendly parties. Lawyers and businessmen sometimes speak of a certain type of concluded contract as being 'open-ended'. By this they mean that although the contract as a whole is to remain unaltered for a term of, say, five years, certain provisions are left open for renegotiation from time to time as conditions change. What we are suggesting is, then, that not only may an explicit contract contain open-ended provisions, but that this quality of open-endedness may at first attach to the interactions of the parties as a whole, which attain a stable meaning only as the reciprocal expectations they engender become fixed through habit and repetition.

Changing the figure somewhat, we may invoke an analogy from the theatre. When we are concerned with the law of an explicit contract, we may say that the lines for the actors have been written out in advance, and in staging the play they are expected to follow the script faithfully, though some licence is necessarily accorded to improvisation when something goes wrong in the course of the performance. Customary law, in contrast, is like a play improvised from the beginning; if in the end it achieves unity and coherence, these qualities are not imposed on it by any single, deliberate decision, but emerge from the interplay of the parts as they are acted out.

In applying these analogies it is, of course, essential to recall that we are throughout dealing with distinctions not of kind but of degree. It is useful to say that explicit contract is a source of made law, if we remember that, like every other form of made law, it will contain an indefinite measure of unverbalized, implicit elements. So, too, we may say that customary law is a form of implicit law, recalling always that there enter into it elements of conscious decision that infuse, rather than dominate, its structure.

So far we have been comparing the processes by which customary and contractual law come into being. What shall we say of the outcome or final product? Does the law that results from what we have called 'open-ended bargaining' – we might also have spoken of an 'oblique kind of bargaining' – differ in characteristic ways from that produced by direct, explicit negotiation?

The first and most obvious observation is that the law of a contract normally differs from customary law by being more *explicit*: its terms are not left to inference, but are 'spelled out' and put into words. This quality of explicitness extends not simply to the law created by the contract, but to other dimensions as well.

With respect to the time when it goes into operation, the law of a contract normally presents no ambiguity. It will ordinarily be understood by the parties that it goes into effect at once, or if there is some postponement, a definite date, including perhaps even the hour of the day, will be stipulated as the time of its effectiveness. A custom, on the other hand, commonly glides into being imperceptibly, as the interactions of the parties come increasingly to express a fixed pattern of reciprocal expectations. As with its birth, so it is with the extinction of a custom: characteristically it does not die suddenly, but gradually fades out of existence. A contract, in contrast, will normally stipulate a definite expiration date. Again, as with the element of time, so it is with the question of the persons affected. A contract normally states clearly who are parties to it and therefore subject to its law. A custom, on the other hand, may or may not spread to persons who had no part in its original creation; often it is difficult to know when this extension by contagion has occurred, and if so, how wide it has become.

All of this may seem to add up to the conclusion that contractual law is definitely superior to customary law. A system of legal rules, we may say, ought to let a man know exactly where he stands; this the law of the contract generally does, and customary law often fails to do. But before passing any final judgement we must reflect that in human relations clarity and explicitness can carry costs as well as advantages. The great advantage of customary law is that in its inception it permits the parties subject to it 'to try it on for fit'. If it does not fit at all, it will normally be abandoned before it has become so firmly fixed that it cannot readily be discarded. If it does not quite jibe with the needs of the situation, it may undergo some reshaping in the later interactions of the parties. It is, in any event, not something rigidly tailored in advance to abstract dimensions, but something capable of accommodating itself to the relationship of the parties as the relationship develops through time.

Contractual arrangements are often enabled to survive the test of time only because they contain an element of unarticulated reciprocity that can adjust itself to contingencies which could not have been foreseen with any precision at the time the contract was entered. Many complicated agreements con-

tain clauses (often relating to quite important matters) that at
the outset seem hopelessly ambiguous, but which acquire definiteness of meaning through the interactions of the parties
as the contract is carried out between them. Indeed, and more
remarkably, it sometimes happens that parties will deliberately
phrase in a vague manner one or more key terms in their
agreement. This they do because they cannot in advance foresee just what kind of reciprocal accommodation on the matters
in issue will best serve their respective interests and advance
their shared desire to achieve a workable frame of collaboration. They leave, as it were, a little clearing for the growth of
customary law in the midst of a forest of meticulously drawn
paragraphs.

These observations add up to the conclusion that where the
desirable future pattern of relations between the parties cannot
confidently be foreseen – or 'foresensed' – the wholly explicit
contract, attempting to cover all contingencies in advance,
may become an inept instrument for ordering human affairs.
Such situations call for the 'open-ended kind of bargaining'
that characterizes the inception of customary law.

There are other situations uncongenial to an ordering by
contract where the difficulty lies not so much in a failure of
foresight as in the nature of the relationship proposed as a
subject for contractual regulation. The relations that do not
readily admit of an ordering by explicit contract are those : (1)
between intimates; (2) between hostile parties; and (3) between
parties standing in a relation of superior and inferior, where
the subject matter under consideration touches on the authority
of the superior. Stated differently, an explicit contract requires
for its successful negotiation and operation that the parties
stand at a certain optimum social distance from one another –
not too near and not too distant – and on such a footing of
equality that a contract between them will not seem to compromise an authority enjoyed by one over the other.

Though contracts or 'deals' within the circle of the family –
between parents and children or between husband and wife –
are not unheard of, they are apt to arouse some puzzlement as
to why those involved have been unable to arrange their affairs

without the crutch of explicit agreement. The way in which our reactions to the use of contract will vary with the context may be conveyed by supposing that we have just learned that two parties, A and B, 'have now begun to negotiate'. If the parties involved are hostile nations or bitter rivals within a government, we may rejoice at this news. If they are husband and wife, we are likely to conclude that this turn of events marks the end of their marriage. Without doubt, important cultural influences come to expression in this matter of judging what kind of human context furnishes appropriate material for contractual regulation. For example, it is probable that most of the world's inhabitants would be shocked to learn that it is not uncommon for an American farmer and his adult sons to operate the family farm under a written agreement not distinguishable from one that might be entered by businessmen wholly unrelated to one another.

That relations of intimacy tend to resist regulation by explicit contract does not mean that they are equally resistant to processes of tacit reciprocity like those that underlie customary law. Indeed, in modern societies we may discern in the relations within a family or between intimate friends many of the features thought to be peculiar to the social ordering of primitive societies. Between friends, for example, we may encounter what in a different context would be regarded as an exchange, here tactfully disguised as distinct and unrelated gestures of one-sided generosity. Within most families there will arise elements of something like customary law, one of the most frequent complaints of children being, 'But I'm not supposed to do that.'

It is often asserted that the most deeply cutting difference between primitive and modern societies lies in the restricted role played by contract in the former. If this observation is understood as referring to the explicit agreement, defining in advance the future relations of the parties, there can be no quarrel with it. But we shall be misled if we suppose that relations of reciprocity of an oblique and open-ended sort are absent from even primitive societies; indeed, it is from just such relations that their basic legal systems develop. To understand the relative absence of explicit agreements in preliterate societies, we need not postulate any mysterious incapacity of the primitive mind to grasp possible advantage of an explicit trade or bargain. We need only remind ourselves that the required context – a certain optimum social distance between the parties – is largely absent in a society organized along familial and tribal lines. Friends and hostile adversaries such a society will know, but the friendly adversary in bargaining will be familiar to it only in restricted contexts, such as periodic markets held in certain locations dedicated to restricted varieties of trade.

Certainly no laboured argument is required to demonstrate that parties openly hostile to one another will find it difficult to subject their relations to control by explicit agreement. But here again man is not without an expedient. Where bargaining with words is impossible, it is often feasible to half-bargain with deeds and forbearances. Out of the imperfect communication thus achieved there may gradually arise a functioning system of customary law. As we have previously observed, it is precisely in curbing destructive hostilities that customary law has historically performed its most important function.

There remains for consideration the third – and final – social context that resists regulation by explicit contract. This is the relation between superior and inferior. The intractability of this relation to regulation by consensual arrangements is only one element of a broader constraint affecting it. Authority always serves in some measure to block communication between those possessing it and those subject to its exercise. The man who wields power over others is apt to fear that a too conspicuous concern for the welfare of those under him may invite inconvenient remonstrances. Even explaining and justifying imposed rules may seem to forfeit for them something of their imperative quality and introduce into the parties' relations an air of friendly counsel. The man subject to authority, on the other hand, hesitates to express his grievances for fear of bringing new restrictions on his head: if he pleads that the rules imposed on him reflect a misconception of his situation, his complaint may reveal to his superiors hitherto overlooked elements in his behaviour that they will consider in need of correction.

His plight is like that of a man who has received a misfitting suit from his tailor and who fears to speak of it, knowing that his tailor has only one way of correcting misfits, that of making the whole suit fit tighter.

Relationships of authority tend to be afflicted, then, by a chronic reciprocity of silence on all matters touching the existence and exercise of the authority itself. Each party to the relationship, ruler and ruled alike, is apt to believe it would be unwise for him to open up a more effective communication. The result is that grievances accumulate and the established rules often become increasingly inept instruments for achieving the purposes towards which they were originally directed. That this situation can be unfavourable to the man subject to authority needs no demonstration. But it is sometimes forgotten that it may also serve badly the interests of him who wields authority. Even in the case of the most degraded of all relations of social power, that of master and slave, the master at least wants his slave to preserve enough health, understanding, and morale so that he can effectively execute the commands given to him. Plainly, well-being is not something that can be effectively projected into the life of another without in some measure drawing him into consultation. In a situation in which tacit restraints have long held back needed readjustment, when the inevitable reckoning finally comes it is apt to be grossly disruptive, accompanied by fumbling manoeuvres on both sides, and shadowed over with the threat of violence.

It may be instructive to consider an example of such an adjustment which has been repeated many times over. Our illustration, to be sure, will not involve the relation of master and slave, but perhaps its closest analogy in modern society. As the result of discontents accumulated over many years, the inmates of a penitentiary suddenly 'go on strike'. They gather together in the dining hall, hold three guards as hostages, refuse to retire to their cells, and demand to meet with someone who can negotiate a settlement. Threats of disciplinary measures by prison officials fail to end the strike. A personal representative of the governor is dispatched to the scene. Before entering the prison he is asked by newspaper reporters whether he intends to reach some kind of agreement with the striking prisoners. The answer is an emphatic 'No'. There will be no bargaining, not even any discussion of grievances, until the prisoners release their hostages and return to their cells. Asked if he will listen to their complaints, the representative answers that this is possible, but that he will in no way 'discuss' those complaints in any manner that would imply negotiation about them.

The governor's representative enters the prison and talks with the convicts for over three hours, at the end of which time they release their hostages and return to their cells. On his emergence the representative is asked if he reached any agreement with the strikers. He answers again with an emphatic 'No'. He is, however, prepared to make certain recommendations to the governor and the prison administration. It soon becomes apparent that although no explicit bargain was struck – the representative was most scrupulous about that – certain reciprocal expectations have been engendered by the long talk that took place. These include an anticipation that certain readjustments will be made in the administration and discipline of the prison. These contemplated changes, originally left vague, gain definiteness as they go into practice and become part of what may properly be called the prison's internal customary law.

Here, then, is another context in which explicit bargaining must give way to the open-ended and oblique kind of bargaining by which customary law comes into being. In this instance there are those who will be appalled by the hypocrisy that seems to be involved. But this hypocrisy – it might better be called studied ambivalence – may have offered the only feasible route to a solution of the prison strike. It should be remembered that the prison authorities have a quite legitimate interest in preventing their relations with inmates from degenerating into daily bargaining sessions. And the inmates, for their part, may have had enough insight to see that their gains were possible only by forgoing any attempt to saddle the authorities with a precedent for explicit bargaining.

The prison strike is one of a class of incidents that may be loosely described as mutinies. Another instance would be the 'wildcat' strike in labour relations – disgruntled workers in a particular department of a factory go on strike contrary to the instructions of their union and in violation of the collective bargaining agreement. Such revolts are generally settled, when a threat of unrestricted disciplinary measures fails, by a tacit readjustment in the expectations of the parties that usually receives only imperfect and indirect expression in the words exchanged between them.

In the discussion just concluded we have devoted some dozen paragraphs to analysing situations in which explicit contract proves an inept instrument for arranging human relationships and where its place must be taken by something like customary law. There remain for brief consideration instances where customary law proves itself capable of overriding the terms of an express agreement. The first such instance scarcely presents any difficulty. This arises when, the performance of a contract taking place over a period of time, the parties silently depart from its terms and govern their conduct towards each other by rules contradicting the language of the contract itself. Here it is easy to say that the contract has been modified by tacit agreement, though it would be equally admissible, and perhaps more realistic, to say that the contract has been over-ridden by a kind of two-party customary law.

Other instances where actions – better, interactions – speak louder than words are less easily disposed of. In a written contract an employer promises the employee at the end of the year a bonus in addition to his regular salary. This promise is accompanied by the words: 'It is expressly understood by the parties hereto that the provision for a bonus herein contained shall impose no legal liability whatsoever on the employer, and that no action at law shall be brought for its recovery, it being understood that the payment of the bonus rests entirely in the uncontrolled discretion of the employer.' There are a considerable number of cases in the United States where courts have ordered the employer to pay the bonus notwithstanding language like that just quoted. However it may be qualified by words, the expectation that the bonus will be paid enters into and conditions the parties' conduct towards one another;

the employee may refrain from asking for a rise, or turn down an offer from another firm, because he is counting on the 'unenforceable' bonus. In short, anticipation of the bonus has taken such deep roots that it becomes an intrinsic part of the employment relation which mere words on paper cannot displace.

There remains for consideration one further infirmity of explicit contract considered as a means of ordering human relations. This lies in an element of ego-involvement that is easily awakened in any protracted negotiation. (It should be recalled that in this discussion, as throughout, we do not have in mind anything like a horse trade, but rather an agreement that serves as a kind of miniature government for the parties' relations, that provides them with a framework for future collaboration or, at worst, with a set of regulations that can serve to set limits to their reciprocal impulses towards destruction.) Negotiation, we may say, ought strictly to be viewed simply as a means to an end; it is the road the parties must travel to arrive at their goal of a mutually satisfactory settlement. But like other means, negotiation is easily converted into an end in itself; it readily becomes a game played for its own sake and a game played with so little reserve by those taken up with it that they will sacrifice their own ultimate interests in order to win it.

It should be recalled that in any complex negotiation the items under consideration are subject to a double evaluation. When, for example, an employer receives from a labour union a demand for an increase in the annual paid vacation granted to his employees, he generally has no way of knowing how this particular concession would be valued by his employees, how they would rate it, for example, in comparison with an increase in pension benefits which they have also asked for in their negotiations. The union, on the other hand, cannot know how much the proposed extension of vacation benefits would actually cost the employer. The employer may customarily take advantage of the vacation period as an occasion for making repairs and alterations in the interior of his factory, and conceivably an extension of the annual shutdown might carry certain advantages partially offsetting its direct monetary cost. On the other hand, the extension of the shutdown might come at a time when it would impair the employer's competitive position and involve serious disadvantages for him. In going into negotiation, then, each party has to take up his starting position on the best calculation he can make of his own interests and his best guess as to the posture of the opposing parties' interests. As the negotiations get under way, readjustments in the positions thus assumed become inevitable as the fitting together of the opposing interests proceeds. If the parties are experienced in negotiation and are genuinely interested in reaching a settlement, these adjustments can be accomplished with a minimum of discomfiture. The situation will be quite otherwise if the parties begin playing the game of negotiation with one another and try to score points on positions taken and positions maintained. In this atmosphere the agreement ultimately reached is likely to be something of a misfit for the interests of both parties. And when in this connection we speak of the baneful effects of ego-involvement it must be remembered that the 'ego' involved may be the most intractable and dangerous of all, not that of an individual, but a curious social phenomenon that may be called the organizational ego.

One of the most astute observers of modern organizational life, Chester Barnard, has some penetrating things to say about the perversions to which negotiation is subject, even in the hands of astute businessmen intent on profit. He writes that in contractual exchange,

... the rule must be that you give, so far as possible, what is less valuable to you but more valuable to the receiver; and you receive what is more valuable to you and less valuable to the giver. This is common sense, good business sense, good social sense, good technology, and is the enduring basis of amicable and constructive relations of any kind. This does *not* mean that you give as little as you can from the *receiver's* point of view.... What conceals this simple fact of experience so often is that subsequent evaluations may change, though this is then beside the point. I may pay a man $10 today with pleasure, and find tomorrow that I need $10 very badly, but cannot use the services I paid for. I am then perhaps disposed to think I made a bad exchange. I read the past into the present. This leads to the false view that what exchange *should* be is as little as possible of what the *receiver* wants, regardless of its value to me. This philosophy of giving as little as possible and getting as much as possible ·in the *other man's values* is the root of bad customer relations, bad labour relations, bad credit relations, bad supply relations, bad technology. The possible margins of cooperative success are too limited to survive the destruction of incentives which this philosophy implies.*

The spirit that will lead a man to accept short measure for himself in order to boast that he at least kept the other fellow from getting what he wanted is by no means confined to business relations. Indeed there is no field more conducive to its growth than international relations. It is, however, a spirit that is engendered by explicit negotiations, where each party is compelled to take his stand – to declare what he wants and what he will give. Here, once more, the less explicit and less verbalized forms of reciprocal adjustment may offer an advantage. If a man is not required to announce that he is shifting his position, he may become more flexible; if he is permitted to pretend that he is not giving anything at all, he may in fact give much – and at the same time serve his own interests more effectively.

In concluding this section, it will be well to recall its title, 'Made elements in implict law', and to bring the discussion into closer relation with that title. For some time we have been concerned with a comparison between customary law and the law created by explicit contract. Both of these forms of law may be said to be 'implicit' in the sense that they develop out of, and respond to, the situation of the parties subject to them, instead of being imposed by some external lawmaker. At the same time, between contract and customary law the 'made' element predominates in the law of the contract, while it plays a less conspicuous role in customary law. That this distinction exists should not blind us to the fact that it is, after all, one of degree. This is a point on which we have repeatedly insisted. The discussion just completed has been predicated on the as-

* *The Functions of the Executive*, Harvard University Press, Cambridge, Mass., 1938, pp. 254–5.

sumption that customary law does not simply 'grow' of its own accord, but that at its inception it expresses a reciprocal adjustment by the affected parties in the expectations each entertains concerning the conduct of the other. It is only when customary law is viewed in this light that it can be appraised as an alternative to explicit contract in the ordering of human affairs, an alternative that in certain contexts is decidedly more effective than contract and, in others, at least more accessible.

It should be recalled that in our discussion we have not been concerned solely with what may be called fully matured customary law – where, in effect, the parties' reciprocal expectations have jelled through repeated interactions – but also with what may be called customary law in the making. The unverbalized accommodations that characterize this incipient stage may be too ephemeral to deserve the name of law, yet they may serve as a kind of scaffolding upon which a more stable order can be built. This is especially so where the initial objective is to avoid open conflict.

Reaching farther back in our discussion, it may be recalled that we have been concerned to show that no single form of social ordering has a first claim to being workable and just, but that there are a number of distinct forms, each with its virtues and defects. Choice among these forms must depend on their aptness for the task at hand and, less obviously, on their availability. In speaking of the 'availability' of forms of social ordering we have in mind such problems as whether a particular form lies within the experience of the parties so as to enter into their repertory of possible responses, as well as the question of 'optimum social distance' discussed in analysing the limitations of contract as a source of social order. In general we have distinguished three distinct forms of social ordering: explicit legislation, contract, and customary law. Each of these has its special advantages and drawbacks and, when closely examined, all present a mixture of 'made' and 'implicit' elements.

It is now time to turn to an institution – 'the common law' – which in modern times is largely identified with the Anglo-American legal system. In examining the common law we shall at the same time be analysing *adjudication* as a distinct source of social order, to be put on the same plane with legislation, contract, and customary law. 'Adjudication' here does not refer to the role of the judge as one who interprets and applies laws enacted by a legislature. Rather we have in mind a system of 'judge-made law', where legal rules for the decision of controversies are not laid down in advance by some external legislative agency, but emerge from the adjudicative process itself.

The common law

First it is necessary to dispose briefly of a problem of nomenclature. European equivalents of the expression 'common law' have been used, especially in Germany, to describe an emergent system of national law, based on the Roman model, that came into existence before national parliaments undertook to enact laws for the nation as a whole. In this use, 'the common law' (*gemeines Recht*) was used to distinguish the commonly shared tradition of Roman law from local statutes and customs. With this usage we are, of course, not concerned here.

Within the English system itself the expression 'the common law' has been used in two senses. In the first of these it refers to judge-made law generally, as distinguished from statutory law; this is of course the sense of the term with which we shall be chiefly concerned. Within the system of judge-made law, however, the expression 'the common law' is used to distinguish between: 1) the law developed through the decisions of 'the common law courts', that is, what may be called 'the regular courts'; and 2) the law emerging from the decisions of a special court known as the court of chancery or 'equity'. 'The courts of the common law' formed the older branch of the judiciary, and their conception of the judicial process was in consequence a restricted one; in general, it excluded that form of relief called 'specific performance' whereby, for example, the successful plaintiff in a suit on a contract secures an order of the court directing the defendant to perform his contract instead of merely being granted monetary relief, which was the standard form of remedy administered by the older 'courts of the common law'. At one time in the Anglo-American system, in order to secure specific performance as well as certain other remedial and substantive advantages, it was necessary to turn to courts of equity. Today, this distinction between two kinds of courts has largely disappeared, and the same judicial system administers both 'equity' and 'the common law'.

A different usage of the term 'common law' comes into play when we distinguish among the legal systems of the various nations. Among the Western countries we distinguish between 'the common law nations' and the 'civil law nations'. In this context, the common law nations are understood to be countries deriving their legal systems from the English model, though in such countries today a considerable portion of the law is, of course, embodied in statutes. The civil law countries, on the other hand, are those deriving their legal traditions, concepts, and vocabularies from ancient Rome. Such countries, it happens, are today characterized by comprehensive codifications, legislatively imposed, from which – in theory at least – the courts derive all the rules by which cases are decided. A civil law country (sometimes called a country of the modern Roman law) does not, then, generally recognize judicial decisions as being of themselves an original source of legal rules. Roughly speaking, among the western nations the common law countries are the English-speaking nations, while the countries of the civil law are those where the prevailing language is not English, but is usually one of the modern derivatives of Latin. Naturally, as with all such distinctions, there are anomalies; for example, a small pocket of civil law maintains itself with moderate success today in Louisiana.

With these distinctions in linguistic usage out of the way, our concern is with the characteristics of what may be called adjudicative law, that is, law incorporated in and derived from judicial decisions, and more particularly with this form of law as it developed in England and then later spread through most of the English-speaking world. We have up to this point followed an established usage in speaking of this kind of law as 'judge-made'. This usage we shall now abandon. One of our chief tasks will be, indeed, to inquire to what extent adjudicative law is in reality what we have called 'made' law and to what extent it exhibits the characteristics of 'implicit' law.

This is a point on which legal scholarship has diverged sharply. The older view, still not entirely abandoned, maintained that the courts do not make law at all, but merely discover or discern it. The opposing view is that the courts just as truly make law as do legislatures; the only difference is that the legislature lays down in advance a general rule, whereas the courts develop general rules gradually in the course of a case-by-case decision of controversies as they are presented for decision.

As for practical lawyers and the courts themselves, it would be fair to say that they have always used, and still use, a kind of double language in describing the judicial function. This phenomenon is described by Maine in the following passage:

We in England are . . . accustomed to the extension, modification, and improvement of law by a machinery (that of the common law) which, in theory, is incapable of altering one jot or one line of existing jurisprudence. The process by which this virtual legislation is effected is not so much insensible as unacknowledged. With respect to that great portion of our legal system which is enshrined in cases and recorded in law reports, we habitually employ a double language, and entertain, as it would appear, a double and inconsistent set of ideas. When a group of facts comes before an English Court for adjudication, the whole course of the discussion between the judge and the advocates assumes that no question is, or can be, raised which will call for the application of any principles but old ones, or of any distinctions but such as have long since been allowed. It is taken absolutely for granted that there is somewhere a rule of known law which will cover the facts of the dispute now litigated, and that, if such a rule be not discovered, it is only that the necessary patience, knowledge, or acumen is not forthcoming to detect it. Yet the moment the judgment has been rendered and reported, we slide unconsciously or unavowedly into a new language and a new train of thought. We now admit that the new decision *has* modified the law. The rules applicable have, to use the very inaccurate expression sometimes employed, become more elastic. In fact they have been changed. A clear addition has been made to the precedents ... The fact that the old rule has been repealed, and that a new one has replaced it, eludes us, because we are not in the habit of throwing into precise language the legal formulas which we derive from the precedents, so that a change in their tenor is not easily detected unless it is violent and glaring. ... We do not admit that our tribunals legislate; we imply that they have never legislated; and yet we maintain that the rules of the English common law, with some assistance from the Court of Chancery and from Parliament, are coextensive with the complicated interests of modern society.*

Maine was writing in 1865 and perhaps overestimated, even for his own day, the capacity of the English bar for illogic. At any rate, since his time there has been a shift towards a more realistic view. Sir Frederick Pollock makes the following comments:

No intelligent lawyer would at this day pretend that the decisions of the Courts do not add to and alter the law. The Courts themselves, in the course of the reasons given for those decisions, constantly and freely use language admitting that they do. Certainly they do not claim legislative power; nor, with all respect for Maine, do they exercise it. For a legislator is not bound to conform to the known existing rules or principles of law; statutes may not only amend but reverse the rule, or they may introduce absolutely novel principles and remedies, like the Workmen's Compensation Act. Still less, if possible, is he bound to respect previous legislation. But English judges are bound to give their decisions in conformity with the settled general principles of English law, with any express legislation applicable to the matter in hand, and with the authority of their predecessors and their own former decisions. At the same time they are bound to find a decision for every case, however novel it may be; and that decision will be authority for other like cases in future; therefore it is part of their duty to lay down new rules if required. Perhaps this is really the first and greatest rule of our customary law: that, failing a specific rule already ascertained and fitting the case in hand, the King's judges must find and apply the most reasonable rule they can, so that it be not inconsistent with any established principle. They not only may but must develop the law in every direction except that of contradicting rules which authority has once fixed. Whoever denies this must deny that novel

* op. cit., pp. 35–9.

combinations of facts are brought before the Courts from time to time, which is a truth vouched by common experience and recognized in the forensic phrase describing such cases as 'of the first impression'; or else he must refuse to accept the principle that the Court is bound to find a decision for every case, however novel. It is true that at many times the Courts have been over-anxious to avoid the appearance of novelty; and the shifts to which they resorted to avoid it have encumbered the Common Law with several of the fictions which Maine denounces ... as almost hopeless obstacles to an orderly distribution of its contents.*

Pollock's comments call for two observations: first, he neglects to remind his reader that although the courts do try hard to fit their decisions into established doctrine, they claim, and on occasion reluctantly exercise, the power to overrule previous decisions. The only exception has been the House of Lords, and even that august tribunal in the summer of 1966 announced that it would henceforth consider itself free to overrule its own precedents. Naturally the power to set aside precedents has always been employed cautiously, though with fluctuations through the centuries between a tightly conservative and a less restricted conception of the matter.

The second observation relates to Pollock's use of the term 'our customary law' as an equivalent for 'the common law'. This has been an accepted usage in England, having been given great currency by Blackstone. The notion back of it is that, just as customary law in the more accustomed sense is found in the practices of laymen, so the common law finds its expression in the practices followed by judges in the decision of cases. Sometimes this identification takes on an almost mystic tone, as when it is suggested by Blackstone that both the practices of laymen and those of judges, when they are rightly inspired, bring to expression something larger than either of them – 'the Law'.

In our previous discussion of made law and implicit law we had occasion to speak of those who like, or dislike 'the intellectual flavour of made law'. This figure was intended to convey the thought that we are here dealing not with ideas of anything

* op. cit., Note D, pp. 46–7.

like geometric precision. but with general inclinations of the mind. Nowhere is this more true than in the debate between those who insist that judges 'make' law just as truly as do legislators and those of the opposite camp, who maintain that the judges merely 'find' or bring to articulate expression something that was already there. Before attempting our own analysis it will be well to get before us some representative expressions from both camps.

As maintaining the view that judges do not make law, we shall present a single champion, Blackstone, who unassisted is quite capable of holding off the opposition, at least if what counts in the struggle is vigour of statement and depth of conviction. His statement is not the less representative because it struggles with a certain inner contradiction afflicting any view which insists, on the one hand, that the judges merely find law, and the patent fact, on the other, that their report of what they have found is conclusive and permits of no challenge:

As to general customs, or the common law, properly so called; this is that law, by which proceedings and determinations in the king's ordinary courts of justice are guided and directed.... How are these customs or maxims to be known, and by whom is their validity to be determined? The answer is, by the judges in the several courts of justice. They are the depositaries of the laws; the living oracles, who must decide in all cases of doubt, and who are bound by an oath to decide according to the law of the land ... it is an established rule to abide by former precedents, where the same points come again in litigation; as well to keep the scale of justice even and steady, and not liable to waver with every new judge's opinion; as also because the law in that case being solemnly declared and determined, what before was uncertain, and perhaps indifferent, is now become a permanent rule, which it is not in the breast of any subsequent judge to alter or vary from, according to his private sentiments, he being sworn to determine, not according to his own private judgement, but according to the known laws and customs of the land; not delegated to pronounce a new law, but to maintain and expound the old one. Yet this rule admits of exceptions where the former determination is most evidently contrary to reason; much more if it be clearly contrary to divine law. But even in such cases the subsequent judges do not pretend to make a new law, but to vindicate the old one from misrepresentation. For if it be found that the former decision is manifestly absurd or unjust, it is declared, not that such a sentence was *bad law*, but that it was *not law* . . .*

Turning to the opposing view, we find an American anthropologist speaking of 'the old self-delusion of Anglo-American juristic dogma that courts do not make law, but only state it and enforce it'. In the same vein Austin had written caustically of

. . . the childish fiction employed by our judges, that judiciary or common law is not made by them, but is a miraculous something made by nobody, existing, I suppose, from eternity, and merely *declared* from time to time by the judges.†

The difficulty with these statements – and their number could be multiplied several times over – is that they are so concerned to tell us what the common law *is*, that they neglect to inform us as to what it is *like*; they are so insistent on discerning its true nature that they forget to analyse the actual processes out of which the common law develops and how those processes differ in fact from those that produce statutory law. There are, in fact, certain rather easily understood considerations affecting those two processes that go far to explain the divergent opinions we have quoted. In the account that follows we shall discern some *ten* differences in the ways by which statutory law and adjudicative law come respectively into being. The matter is, however, by no means so complicated as that number would suggest, for the differences we shall set forth are closely interrelated, so that they bring to expression what are in part distinct aspects of a single, fundamental cleavage.

First. Adjudicative law emerges from the decision of actual controversies; it does not lay down rules in advance for the decision of cases, but waits for controversies to be brought before the court for decision. Statutes, in contrast, lay down general rules in anticipation of cases yet to arise. Occasionally, to be sure, the origin of a particular statute can be traced to some single incident that brought to light a defect in the existing law. But where this occurs, the statute will generally leave

* *Commentaries*, Book I, Rees Welch & Co., Philadelphia, 1897, pp. 68–70.

† op. cit., vol. ii, p. 655.

unaffected the case that gave rise to it, in accordance with the rule against retrospective laws, a rule either considered as an implicit restraint on the legislative process or explicitly imposed by a written constitution.

In the case of an incident of the sort just supposed, if the legislature cannot find any satisfactory general formula for controlling similar cases in the future, it may refrain from legislating altogether and leave the problem presented unsolved. No such escape is open to the common law court; it *must* decide the case before it and do the best it can in finding some intelligible principle on which to rest its decision.

The sociologist Max Weber was convinced that in the Anglo-American system of common law 'the degree of legal rationality is essentially lower than, and of a type different from, that of continental Europe'. Perhaps part of what Weber had in mind was that laws are made most rationally when men lay down rules in advance of actual disputes, while their minds are free from the pull of circumstance and person. On the other hand, in complex human affairs it can be argued that to legislate wisely one must acquire some firsthand feeling for the situations about which one is legislating, and that for this reason the common law is likely to be more intelligently responsive to the needs of society than abstract codification. As is often the case, these divergent opinions reflect different aspects of a complex reality and there is truth in both of them.

Second. In a judicial decision under the common law, the *rule* applied to the case and the *reason* or justification for that rule are both stated in the opinion of the judge and are often intertwined to such a point that it is difficult to distinguish between them. A statute, on the other hand, normally contains no argumentative or justificatory statement; it simply asserts: this is forbidden, this is required, this is authorized. If the citizen seeks an explanation for the rules applied to him, he will have to consult the record of the parliamentary debates that gave rise to the statute or, occasionally, the recommendations of some legislative committee that considered the matter in question and had perhaps held public hearings on it. Whether, when a court is applying a statute, it should attempt to resolve ambiguities by recourse to its 'legislative history' is a debated matter. Certainly it is asking much of the citizen to expect him not merely to know what the statute says but to familiarize himself with the legislative deliberations and arguments by which the statute came to say what it does. If the citizen is entitled to take the statute at face value, without a protracted study of its origins, then the court in applying the statute to the citizen ought generally to take a similar view of it.

Though, as we have indicated, the text of a statute does not normally attempt any explanation of the reasons for its enactment, an exception exists in the case of those statutes preceded by a preamble, usually reciting the inconveniences or evils the statute is intended to correct. Just what use a court applying a statute ought to make of such a preamble is, again, a disputed point. Sometimes it is suspected that the preamble is a way of covering up careless draftsmanship; the legislature says, in effect, 'We may not have expressed very well just *what* we want, but you can figure this out for yourself by reading the preamble which tells you *why* we want it.' This use of the preamble moves away from telling the citizen what he must do and towards telling him how he must think; it says in effect, 'If you will participate in our objectives and think as we do about them, then you will know what to do without our having to define your duties too precisely.' In cases where the problems to be solved require a flexible approach, and where there exists among the members of society a strong sense of common interest, then there may be no objection to this procedure, except that carrying it very far would mean the abandonment of a legal order in favour of a regime of managerial direction.

In this connection it is significant that the countries of the Communist bloc make a very free use of the statutory preamble, even the most insignificant-seeming ordinance commonly being preceded by an elaborate explanation of the evils it is intended to correct, a statement that it owes its enactment to the continued influence of reactionary forces in the management of industry, etc. In such cases it is evident that the legislator intends not only to impose on the citizen obligations to act or forbear in certain ways, but to give direction to his thinking as well – something that makes good sense within a managerial or inspirational context, but that can give rise to some disquietude as part of an order declaring legal rights and duties.

The perplexities aroused when a legislature provides an official explanation for its enactments have never afflicted the common law. Its courts have always taken it for granted that they must explain and justify their decisions, that they must demonstrate that the rules they apply are 'grounded in principle'. Fortunately, they have also generally taken it for granted that their task is to lay down rules of law and not to issue managerial directions or to indulge themselves in sermonizing. It is true that the exact nature of the citizen's duties will often be left in some obscurity by the decisions, but, in theory at least, when the obscurity has been lifted what will be revealed is an assertion about what the citizen must do or refrain from doing and not a command to think right or to work cooperatively toward some imposed goal.

Third. The fact that judicial decision is always an *explained* thing means that the interpretation of it is quite different from the interpretation of a statute. Typically in a judicial opinion the rule applied and the reasons justifying it will be seen as two aspects of a single reasoning process. A later court confronted with a decision as a precedent may discern a discrepancy between the decision itself and the justification given for it; it may accept the decision and at the same time assert that the principle on which it was grounded requires reformulation or, moving in the opposite direction, it may accept the previous court's statement of the principle but assert that it was misapplied in the decision actually reached. If a court gives three reasons for its decision, a later court may declare the first reason sound, the second misconceived, and the third a makeweight without real relevance to the problem presented. All of these things can happen within a framework that presupposes the binding force of previous decisions and demands a certain ceremonious civility in the expression of criticisms directed toward their reasoning: 'I have concluded that my learned brother was mistaken in the ground on which he rested his opinion. Had the case before him been such as to attract to his attention the aspect of the problem we are here examining, I am certain he would have given a quiet different explanation for his decision.'

The qualities just suggested have sometimes been expressed by saying that the common law, despite the fact that it is to be found in the printed reports of judicial decisions, is in reality a species of 'unwritten law'. In discussing this usage Maine is guilty of one of his rare lapses of discernment:

English case-law is sometimes spoken of as unwritten, and there are some English theorists who assure us that if a code of English jurisprudence were prepared, we should be turning unwritten law into written – a conversion, as they insist, if not of doubtful policy, at all events of the greatest seriousness.... As soon as the Courts at Westminster Hall began to base their judgments on cases recorded ... the law which they administered became written law. At the present moment a rule of English law has first to be disentangled from the recorded facts of adjudged printed precedents, then thrown into a form of words, varying with the taste, precision, and knowledge of the particular judge, and then applied to the circumstances of the case for adjudication. But at no stage of this process has it any characteristic which distinguishes it from written law. It is written case-law, and only different from code-law because it is written in a different way.*

Maine's own description of the manner in which judicial precedents are interpreted, or 'disentangled', is more than enough to indicate that any attempt to restate the common law in the form of a code would indeed be a 'conversion' of the 'greatest seriousness'. In the common law it is not too much to say that the judges are always ready to look behind the words of a precedent to what the previous court was trying to say, or to what it would have said if it could have foreseen the nature of the cases that were later to arise, or if its perception of the relevant factors in the case before it had been more acute. There is, then, a real sense in which the written words of the reported decisions are merely the gateway to something lying behind them that may be called, without any excess of poetic licence, 'unwritten law'.

* op. cit., pp. 11–12.

Fourth. In the common law the opinion supporting the decision of the court is normally signed by the judge who wrote it. This practice usually comes as a surprise and even as something of a shock to those raised in the traditions of the civil law. A statute or code carries no signature; it speaks, as it were, out of a corporate void. In the general practice of the civil law countries the judicial opinions interpreting statutes are also anonymous.

In the practice of the signed opinion Weber discerned further evidence for the conclusion that the common law represents a kind of legal rationality 'essentially lower than, and of a type different from, that of continental Europe'. He spoke indeed of the judicial process in the Anglo-American countries as taking on a 'charismatic quality' and as resting on 'the very personal authority' of the 'individual judge'. Yet in most fields of intellectual activity it would be taken for granted that in difficult or doubtful matters one man's opinion carries more weight than that of others; no quality of 'irrationality' or superstitious awe of the person would be seen in the simple conclusion that 'on this matter A is a better guide than B', or 'A is better at explaining these things than B'.

If similar expressions applied to signed judicial decisions cause alarm or discomfort, it is because we are looking at law from the outside, as a 'made' or finished product, instead of participating vicariously in the processes of deliberation and discussion that brought it into being. It does, to be sure, sound odd to say that 'Judge A makes better law than Judge B'. Yet if one could be admitted into the deliberations of a parliamentary drafting committee engaged in 'making' statutory law, one would scarcely be surprised to be told quietly that 'in the planning and drafting of statutes Legislator A shows more judgement, foresight, and skill than does Legislator B'. The judges of the common law do their legislative drafting, as it were, in public or at least within the full view of their colleagues. The law they 'make' is not viewed by the judges who come after them as a finished thing, but as something to be reformulated and improved in the light of experience and sober second thought, in the same way that a statute can often, after it has been in force for a time, be improved by amendment. And just as a legislator might stay his hand before rewriting the text of a statute drafted by an acknowledged master, so a judge will accord a varying deference to the work accomplished by his predecessors, not only in the reaching of their decisions but in explaining and justifying them.

To appreciate the role of the signed opinion in the common law one must realize that 1) the task of phrasing apt and just rules of law for the shifting contingencies of life is a difficult undertaking, as is also that of explaining those rules or giving them a proper 'grounding in principle'; 2) in the common law system this task is thought of as a collaborative enterprise extending through time in which many judges will participate. Within such a frame of reference it will be readily understood that the contribution of individual judges will inevitably and properly be appraised in view of their wisdom, their capacity to give effective verbal expression to that wisdom, their acquaintance with the area of life affected by a particular decision, and many other 'personal' qualities.

Fifth. In the common law not only is the opinion of a unanimous court normally signed by the judge who wrote it, but on occasion there will be a signed *dissenting* opinion or, less frequently, a signed *concurring* opinion, the occasion for the latter arising when the concurring judge agrees with the majority decision but disapproves in some particular of its reasoning. There may also be combinations of these forms of judicial self-expression, such as an opinion concurring in a dissent registered by another judge. Finally, and expressing the epitome of the common law spirit, there is the opinion entered *dubitante* – the judge is unhappy about some aspect of the decision rendered, but cannot quite bring himself to record an open dissent. The reader will realize that these variant forms of judicial expression represent distinct strands of thought that may be taken up by later judges and rewoven into a pattern that diverges somewhat from anything previously discernible in the decisions.

The institution of multiple opinions has an important bearing on any appraisal of the doctrine of *stare decisis* – the prin-

ciple by which the common law courts generally purport 'to
stand by the thing decided' and render to established precedent
its due. To abide by a precedent turns out not to be so onerous
a thing if the precedent looks in several directions at once. The
decision of the House of Lords to abandon its rule that it
would never overrule a precedent was thus by no means so
revolutionary an action as it might seem, for it was no accident
that the Law Lords have always been accustomed, even in
unanimous decisions, to deliver lengthy individual opinions.
These opinions seldom see quite eye-to-eye on the issues involved in any case or on the proper way of explaining the
principle exemplified in the decision. The somewhat divergent
signposts thus set up by separate explanations of what is being
decided obviously accord a considerable freedom of action to
later courts, even within the restraints of a rule which declares
that precedents must invariably be followed.

Sixth. In contrast with the practice of other legal systems, the
printed reports of judicial decisions in the common law normally set forth, in very considerable detail, the *facts* of the cases
being decided; these reports, in other words, tell a relatively
complete story of what happened before the case came to court.
This lends to the law reports a certain human interest but often
puzzles continental lawyers who wonder why the report of a
case should not confine itself to those facts which are directly
relevant to the decision as that decision is explained by the
judges themselves. It would be easy to discern in the common
law practice an expression of the pragmatic bent of the Anglo-
American mind, often supposed to be interested in 'facts' but
unconcerned with 'principle'.

In truth, however, a relatively complete statement of the
facts of the case being decided is an intrinsic demand of the
system of legal thought represented by the common law. As
we have pointed out, in applying a precedent a later court may
accept its result, but reject the explanation of that result; it
may approve the principle enunciated, but declare it to have
been misapplied in the case actually decided. As reasons, principles, and explanations shift, so does the relevance of particular facts; a truncated factual statement, cut to fit a particular

theory of the case, would ill serve the process of growth and rearticulation that is an essential characteristic of the common law.

Seventh. Those responsible for creating and administering a body of legal rules will always be confronted by a *problem of system*. The rules applied to the decision of individual controversies cannot simply be isolated exercises of judicial wisdom. They must be brought into, and maintained in, some systematic interrelationship; they must display some coherent internal structure.

This is a requirement of justice itself. In its most rudimentary expression, justice demands the like decision of like cases. Since no two cases are ever exactly alike, one cannot act justly unless one is able to define what constitutes an essential likeness. But to discern what is essential and what is not in the decision of a case, one must have resort to principles that transcend their immediate application; it is these general principles that bind the elements of law into a coherent system of thought.

In the civil law countries, system is thought of as a problem to be solved, once and for all, by the legislator in the form he gives to statutory law. In the common law countries, on the other hand, system is a problem for the judge and the task of solving it forms a part of his daily routine; it is scarcely an exaggeration to say that for the common law, in the hands of the Anglo-American judge, system is a problem never solved, but always in the process of being solved.

In the common law the problem of system stands in close relation to two of its most obvious and most commonly noted characteristics: first, its rules are not laid down in advance, but develop out of actual cases as the accidents of litigation may bring them up for decision; second, the common law has a strong penchant for following established precedents. The first of these characteristics is related to the problem of system as lending to it a special quality not found in statutory law; the second stands toward the problem of system as an element in its solution.

The predicament of the common law judge, who cannot make rules in advance, but must wait for the cases to come to him, suggests the analogy of a builder attempting to construct a house with no control over the arrival of his materials, so that the shingles come before the foundation stones and the chimney bricks arrive on the site before the flooring. To the extent that this figure is apt it may truly be said that the common law is forced into a very messy way of building its house of legal doctrine. Fortunately, the plight of the judge is not quite so serious as this figure might suggest. The important and basic problems have a habit of coming up for decision at an early point; what we have described as 'the accidents of litigation' will tend at least toward a random distribution of the issues submitted for judicial determination; and, finally, swings of the pendulum of history will bring it about that at any given time the judiciary will be preoccupied with issues of pressing current interest and those issues will tend to be closely interrelated. With all these allowances, it still remains true that the problems of achieving and maintaining some systematic order in the law is a very different one for the judge of the common law than it is for the judge who has at his elbow, as the cases come before him for decision, a comprehensive, ready-made code.

It is often assumed that the common law penchant for following precedent is simply an expression of the innate conservatism of the legal profession and of its distaste for change of any sort. This view distorts a complex issue and obscures the nature of the judge's task. That it cannot be the whole truth of the matter is clear if we recall two quite inconsistent criticisms that are commonly made of the way judges of the common law treat precedents: 1) it is said that they adhere woodenly to precedent in the face of changing social conditions; 2) it is said that they pretend hypocritically to follow precedent but in fact reinterpret and distinguish it in so free a measure as to destroy its real force as a standard of decision.

These conflicting views may be reconciled if we think of a precedent as offering to later judges not simply a place of common anchorage but also a shared point of embarkment towards new law. One may often accord respect to a precedent not by embracing it with a frozen logic but by drawing from its thought the elements of a new pattern of decision. The precedents become, under this view, like a common language; they preserve those systematic elements of the law without which communication between generations of lawyers, and among lawyers of the same generation, would be impossible. At the same time, while they may direct the course of change, they impose no unbreachable obstacle to it.

These observations suggest that into the interpretation of precedents there may enter something like an artistic element. In his creative role the judge is, indeed, not unlike the poet who respects the inheritance of his native language in the very act of exploiting its resources for novel uses. Yet in speaking of the judge's creative role, we must not forget the restraints that surround him. Even the most manipulative mind will soon discover that there are intrinsic limits to the process of 'drawing new law out of the old books'. The common law judge, as we have pointed out before, is forced to do his sums in public and under the scrutiny of a conservative profession. Finally, the last word on innovative decisions rests with appellate courts, which are normally collegial in composition and require, therefore, a majority vote of, say, five or seven judges for a final decision.

Eighth. As a kind of symbolic expression of the qualities we have been passing in review, a matter of linguistic usage should be noted: the expression 'the common law' is always used with the definite article and in the singular. Anglo-American lawyers speak of rules, principles, standards, maxims, and precepts *of* the common law, but not of common laws or of *a* common law.

A college textbook in sociology, in introducing its readers to 'the relationships of folkways, mores, and laws', thus describes an alleged usage of the legal profession in speaking of 'common laws':

This label refers to norm definitions which have developed in an informal manner but which have become so well established and intermeshed with formal laws that formal sanctions may be utilized to enforce them. The fact that formal sanctions may be used in enforcement efforts, means, however, that the common laws will be specifically stated in records such as court decisions and thus these norm definitions do take on at least a semi-formal status.

Being familiar with statutory laws. the author of this passage has mistakenly assumed that legal rules of whatever kind can be described as 'laws'. Misled by the words 'common law' he has also confused the common law with customary law and has apparently merged the two into one concept, violating usage still further by assuming that the rules of customary law may be called 'laws'.

There would be no point in insisting on these niceties of juristic usage if they did not bring to expression fundamental aspects of the processes by which law and laws come into being. We are all prone to think of a statutory law as a made thing, that can be understood in abstraction from the way it came into being and from the larger system of which it forms a part. There is, of course, a danger that even in this case the language we use may distract attention from what have been previously described as 'implicit elements in made law'. But a risk that is bearable when we are thinking of enacted law becomes altogether unacceptable when our minds are directed toward the rules that emerge from the procedures of the common law. If we were to adopt the habit of describing 'a rule of the common law' as 'a common law' we might soon forget that to understand this 'law' we must see it in the context of a larger system of thought of which it is a part.

Ninth. Laymen and legal philosophers alike have often thought of law as being something like a command or order, issued by the state and directed to the citizen. Austin explicitly defined a law as a command and the law as a system of commands. Now if we start with this conception of law and laws, the following questions will arise quite naturally: Who has the authority to issue these commands? To whom are they addressed? Over what persons and over what territory are they obligatory?

The historical fact is that in the building of the common law these questions have not been given a central place in legal reasoning; where an attempt has been made to answer them, the answer has often been imprecise. To be sure, the question, 'Who is bound by a particular order of court, issued in a particular litigation?' has to be answered as precisely as possible, and the common law has always sought rules that will yield such an answer. But such an order or command, being addressed to a particular person and with respect to a special situation, was not in Austin's system a law at all, but simply an exercise of authority taking the form of an 'occasional or particular command'. Law, properly so called, consisted for Austin of *general* commands, obligating 'to acts or forebearances of a class'. In taking this distinction Austin was, of course, following ordinary usage; we do not call a court order that Jones pay his ex-wife an alimony of $200 a month 'a law', though we assume the order was issued by the court pursuant to law, that is, pursuant to general rules governing such cases and defining the powers of the court.

The judges of the common law have always drawn their general rules of law from a variety of sources and with a rather free disregard for political and jurisdictional boundaries. Saskatchewan may cite a precedent from New South Wales, Vermont may derive guidance from the law propounded by the judges of Arkansas, while the Queen's Bench may find a decision of the Supreme Court of the United States persuasive, or at least helpful, in deciding a case of contract law.

Judges who thus habitually borrow legal wisdom back and forth across political boundaries are apt to talk as if they were all working together in bringing to adequate expression a pre-existing thing called 'The Law'. Plainly this usage will not be readily accepted by those who insist on preserving a sharp distinction between law after it has been made by proper authority and the intellectual ingredients that went into its making. So we find Austin, in a passage cited before,* speaking of the 'childish fiction employed by our judges, that judiciary or common law is not made by them, but is a miraculous something made by nobody'.

Yet it is plain that this 'childish fiction' has greatly facilitated communication and commerce among the nations of the common law. By acting as if there existed a body of legal principle

* See p. 126.

that could be called simply 'The Law', they have brought into existence something not wholly undeserving of that name. And even the notion that the law can, in some sense, pre-exist its declaration by the judges will not seem wholly absurd if we assume that the wisdom which originally shaped it does not forfeit its force and meaning the moment it is reduced to an 'authoritative' verbal statement in a judicial opinion.

What has just been said suggests that the common law system of legal thought is conducive to a unity of legal doctrine among the states or nations that have adopted it. There is, however, at least one element of the system capable of working in the opposite direction. We have several times spoken of the fact that the courts of the common law do not lay down their rules in advance, but develop them out of litigated cases. This inevitably means that the shape taken by legal doctrine in a particular jurisdiction will be influenced by the accidents of litigational history within that jurisdiction.

Let us examine how this factor may work toward a diversity of legal doctrine. A particular rule, we may call it Rule A, is proposed as a standard for deciding a certain class of cases. Now it is a familiar device of casuistry to 'test' the proposed rule by putting a series of hypothetical cases running along a spectrum of increasing embarrassment for those upholding the rule. The first case is easy and shows the rule to excellent advantage; as we move toward the opposite end of the spectrum, however, it becomes increasingly difficult to defend the rule, until finally the breaking point is reached when a case is proposed that would receive an outrageous decision if the rule were applied to it. If, on the other hand, we start with Rule B, the direction of the spectrum may be reversed; the situations most suited for solution by Rule B may be precisely those where the opposing rule would work its most obvious injustice.

So it is that a diversity of legal doctrine may result from the order in which cases happen to come up for decision within different jurisdictions. Thus, we may find that Massachusetts and Tennessee follow Rule A, while California and Illinois follow Rule B. An amateur in anthropology might be tempted to explain this diversity by some recondite cultural influence operative among the populations of Massachusetts and Tennessee, but absent in California and Illinois. In fact the explanation may lie in the simple accident that the earliest cases to come up for decision in the first two states put Rule A in a good light, while in the other two states it was Rule B that seemed most apt for the cases actually presented in litigation. Often with the passage of time this kind of diversity will cure itself; as the cases litigated in all four states begin to display their diverse qualities, the states following Rule A are likely to modify their law in the direction of Rule B, while in the opposing states qualifications and exceptions may develop in the opposite direction. And, plainly, if states pay enough attention to one another's law in the first place, this sort of diversity may never arise, the courts of each state being able to draw on the legal experience of the others.

Tenth. We come now finally to the characteristic of the common law that has caused the most embarassment to its friends and apologists. This lies in the fact that the law laid down in its decisions operates *retrospectively*. This has traditionally been the case even where the judges overrule a precedent that had been accepted for years as settled law. In Blackstone's words, the overruled precedent is treated not as 'bad law' in need of correction for the future, but as 'not law' at all and never having been law, even though thousands of citizens may have relied on it as the only official statement of their rights and duties. Retrospective effect is, of course, also normally given to the reinterpretation of precedents or to decisions projecting legal restraints for the first time into areas previously considered as unregulated by law.

Since the passage of *ex post facto* laws by parliamentary assemblies is, under most circumstances, regarded as a flagrant abuse of legislative power, the question is raised whether judicial 'lawmaking' should be viewed any differently. In attempting an answer to that question we must begin by taking a commonplace distinction between the *making* of laws and their *interpretation*. Where statutory law is concerned, this distinction is, on the surface at least, easy to apply and expresses itself in a division of labour between distinct institutions: the *making* of laws is for the *legislature*, their *interpretation* is for the *judiciary*. In the common law this distinction is not readily discerned; the judges who interpret the law are also those whose decisions brought it into being. Furthermore, and more fundamentally, it is often difficult to say whether a particular judgment of a court creates new law or simply derives its standards of decision from implications already contained in existing law.

If, then, we are to form an intelligent opinion concerning the retrospective effect of judicial decisions, we must begin with a kind of law that permits a more confident distinction between law making and law interpreting (this means, of course, with statutory law). Now the surprising thing is that so far as the judicial interpretation of statutes is concerned, a retrospective effect is normally taken for granted and is scarcely regarded as presenting any problem at all. This is true both in the civil law countries and with respect to statutory law in the common law countries.

This ready acceptance, where a statute is concerned, of the retrospective effect of judicial interpretation would be quite understandable if we could regard the court as simply drawing from the words of the statute an implication that was already plainly there and obvious to any reflective citizen. But this is far from being the case. For one thing, obvious points of interpretation are seldom taken to court; usually it is the doubtful cases that come to litigation. Furthermore, the retrospective effect of judicial interpretation is ordinarily accepted even though it alters a meaning previously attributed to the statute and regarded as settled law. The same holds where a statutory provision is so vague that its coverage can scarcely be defined until it has been judicially interpreted, so that the effective meaning of the statute in reality proceeds from the judiciary and not from the legislature.

Why, then, is the covert lawmaking implicit in the act of interpretation regarded as being exempt from the taboo against retrospective laws? To answer this question we have to consider, as with many problems in the design and operation of social institutions, whether there exists any acceptable alternative. No system of rules can be made so clear that it applies itself; the unforeseen variety thrown up by the contingencies of life will always produce embarrassment from the most carefully drafted regulations. To make workable a system of enacted rules there must be provided, therefore, some machinery of authoritative interpretation that can decide, when a dispute arises between A and B concerning the meaning of a rule, which one of the two is right. Plainly if the result of their litigation were an interpretation that was operative prospectively and for future controversies only, then the whole purpose of providing a means for securing an authoritative resolution of pending disputes would be thwarted. When men quarrel about what the law means and go to court about it, they anticipate an answer to their own quarrel and not a decision solving some similar quarrel between hypothetical future litigants.

It might be argued that while what has just been said applies well enough to normal or routine cases of disputed language, it should not apply to cases where the outcome of a resort to litigation is an interpretation that departs radically from what might be called normal expectations, or where the court overrules a previously established judicial interpretation – where, in other words, there is an element of surprise in the outcome. In such cases, it may be argued, a retrospective effect should not be attributed to the interpretation, which should operate prospectively only and for cases arising after its pronouncement.

But in most cases this solution would only compound the difficulties. To the perplexity of the citizen and his lawyer in trying to guess how a court will interpret a statutory rule, there would be added another dimension of uncertainty: Will the court make its interpretation retrospective or prospective? From any point of view there would be great difficulty in distinguishing between routine and drastic interpretations or reinterpretations. A court that considers its interpretation plainly correct will scarcely incline toward regarding it as drastic or surprising. Sometimes it is easier to predict what might be called a drastic reinterpretation than one moving within a more conventional ambit; this might be true, for example, where an established interpretation had caused such dissatisfaction that it was widely regarded as mistaken and in need of correction. Here the outcome of an appeal to the judiciary for a new interpretation might in fact be more predictable than an interpretation that is necessitated by some curious and nonrecurring set of facts, where a retrospective effect would be taken for granted.

Furthermore, to arrive at a rounded perspective of the problem we must view adjudication as a collaborative process of decision in which the litigant plays an essential role. It is often forgotten that a judicial judgment is not simply a determination made by an official bound by oath to act impartially. It is also the product of a procedure in which the litigant is assured of an opportunity to present proofs and arguments for a decision in his favour. If the litigant is to participate meaningfully in the process of adjudication he must know in advance towards what end that process is directed. If he presents his arguments and proofs without knowing how they will be used by the court, then in effect their essential meaning is determined only after his presentation has been closed.

This would, indeed, be the effect if, when a dispute over the meaning of a statute was brought to court, it was decided only after all the evidence and arguments were presented whether the decision was to be retrospective, and hence govern the case at hand, or prospective and therefore without effect on the immediate case. In the first instance, the arguments and proofs would be presented within a framework of the expectations that normally attend a law suit. In the second, what appeared as a law suit between two litigants would turn out to be, in effect, a legislative hearing addressed to the question whether an existing rule of law stood in need of amendment for the future – a proceeding that may require a different kind of proof and argument, and be of interest to different persons, than that in an ordinary litigation. To postpone determining what the issue was under consideration until the adversaries had presented their respective cases would be like declaring trumps after the hands had been played, and it would, ironically, visit within the procedural framework of the litigation itself the evils of a retrospective enactment of the standards by which the arguments of the parties have to be guided.

Finally, we must keep in mind the social role performed by the litigant. He believes, let us say, that a statute has hitherto been interpreted in a way that is improper and unjust; he challenges the accepted interpretation and takes his challenge to court. If he is found to be right, he has performed a public service in securing a judicial reinterpretation of the statute. It would be a curious way of rewarding this service if, when he brought his case to court, he succeeded in having the rule changed for the future but had the old and now discredited rule applied to his own case. When all these considerations are taken into account, the retrospective effect of judicial interpretations will be seen as an essential element in a system designed to provide a mechanism by which disputes concerning the meaning of statutes can be finally resolved between the disputants.

We began the discussion of statutory interpretation just concluded by observing that in this area of the law there *seemed* to be a clear-cut distinction between the making of laws (which is for the legislature) and the interpretation of law (which is for the courts). Yet our analysis has shown that this distinction breaks down when we consider how much of the meaning of a statute derives not from the words enacted by the legislature, but from a judicial gloss imposed on those words. The true distinction is not that courts interpreting statutes do not 'legislate' at all, but that, in comparison with legislative assemblies, they perform their function within a different institutional framework, by different procedures, and with a different kind of participation accorded to those who are affected by their decisions.

The lessons implicit in our analysis of the role of the judiciary in interpreting statutes should warn us against accepting uncritically such statements as, 'The courts of the common law make law just as truly as do legislative assemblies and they do it in a way no legislature would ordinarily dare, that is, *ex post facto*.' In reality the common law courts 'make' their law, as do courts interpreting statutes, within an institutional context where in the run of cases a retrospective effect is and should be taken for granted. Furthermore, any attempt to separate for special treatment unusual cases where a retrospective determination might work special hardship would itself carry a heavy cost in the confusion it would introduce into the role of the litigant and the function of the court. The retrospective effect normally attributed to judicial decisions in the common law is, then, not some freakish outcropping of that system, but an intrinsic part of any procedure designed to enable parties to present their disputes about the law for an official determination of the legal relationship in which they stand toward one another.

Nothing of what has just been said is intended to deny that the retrospective effect of common law decisions is at times capable of working serious hardship. That hardship can be said to be mitigated by at least four circumstances. First, the respect accorded to precedents in the common law and the reluctance to overrule them reduces the likelihood that the judiciary will indulge in radical and unexpected departures from existing law. Indeed, the courts' adherence to precedent derives much of its motivation from a desire not to impose the hardships that would result from retrospective changes in the law. Seen in this light, the judicial reluctance to overturn established law is an essential part of an integrated system and not simply, as is so often assumed, the expression of some blind aversion to change. Second, when, for reasons just suggested, the court leaves in effect rules that are in need of change, it can – with varying degrees of confidence – rely on the legislature to enact the appropriate corrections. Unlike the court, the legislature can accomplish this task within the normal expectations that encompass its activities. Third, the common law has now largely been purged of one of the harshest aspects of retrospectivity, that affecting the criminal law.

In most jurisdictions where the common law exists the whole of the criminal law has been removed from its reach and entrusted to the legislature. This means that in these jurisdictions no new crimes can be created by judicial decision. Fourth, the countries where the common law system prevails have been countries where there is a considerable unanimity on legal and political issues; in other words, there is not likely to exist any deep-cutting discrepancy between legal standards and general notions of what is fitting and just. In such a social context retrospective changes in the law by judicial decision often serve to bring legal rules into line with general opinion and are therefore not seen as oppressive.

Before quitting the problem of retrospective lawmaking, three supplementary observations are in order. The first relates to a few cases in the United States where retrospective effect has been denied to decisions radically changing previous law. These cases chiefly relate to the liability of hospitals for the negligence of nurses and physicians in their employ. Traditionally, charitable corporations have been exempt in the common law from liability for the negligent acts of their employees. This rule has been widely considered as outmoded, and in some states has been changed by statute. In a number of states it has been overturned by judicial decision. In some instances the new judge-made rule was made entirely prospective, so that even the litigant whose arguments helped to bring about the change in the law had the old rule applied to his case. In other instances the benefit of the new rule was extended to the litigant before the court, even though the facts of his case arose, of necessity, before the new rule was declared; other litigants with claims which arose before the change in the law were, however, denied the benefit of the new rule. The second solution works the obvious injustice of an unlike treatment of like cases, an injustice that will appear as compounded when we take into account that other litigants may have had their cases on the way to the Supreme Court when the crucial case was decided, and only failed to get there first because of accidents in the operation of the court calendar. The first solution could scarcely fail to embitter the litigant whose initiative brought about a major and beneficial legal reform, yet whose only reward is that of going down in the books as the unsuccessful plaintiff in *Doe* v. *The First Parish Hospital*. Back of the judicial predicament that gave rise to this bizarre situation lay a realization that to make the new rule broadly retrospective would let loose a ruinous flood of litigation on institutions that were supported by charitable contributions and that had conducted their affairs in reliance on the old rule and had neglected to take out the insurance appropriate under the new rule.

Our second observation relates to what has been called the 'institutional litigant'. There are organized groups, such as labour unions or trade associations, that have a continuing interest in the development of the common law. A group of this sort may take a case to litigation, not so much for the sake of a determination of the case itself, but for the purpose of bringing about a change in the law or of defending an existing rule against a change sought by some other group. When such groups are involved, the usual arguments against prospective changes in the law through judicial decisions lose much of their force. Indeed, when the litigants have this sort of long-term interest, a judicial proceeding may take on, with the assent of all involved, something of the nature of a legislative hearing. The analogy to such a hearing becomes even stronger when the brief *amicus curiae* is employed; this institutional practice permits a party not actually involved as a litigant to apply to the court for consent to file a written statement as a 'friend of the court'. In such a statement he will set forth his views as to the proper rule to be applied in cases like that under consideration by the court.

Our final observation relates to the effect in the United States of restraints contained in written constitutions. In all jurisdictions the ex post facto criminal statute is unconstitutional and void; the legislature is powerless to make acts criminal that were not so when they were committed. Furthermore, a statute creating a crime in terms so indefinite that it is difficult to know just what acts are prohibited may be declared unconstitutional, there being an established principle of 'unconstitutional vagueness'. This principle may prevent the situation from arising where in avoiding criminal acts men can obtain no real guidance from the words of the statute, but must have the criminality of their conduct, or the lack of it, determined by retrospective judicial interpretation. Finally, a retrospective change in the interpretation of a statute has been proscribed in cases like the following: The legislature enacts a criminal statute that is reasonably subject to two interpretations: by one interpretation (the more restrictive) the statute proscribes acts *a*, *b*, and *c*; by a more extensive interpretation, act *d* is also prohibited. As an original proposition either interpretation would have been regarded as proper. Suppose, however, that in the first cases to arise the court has attributed a restrictive meaning to the statute, so that it covers only acts *a*, *b*, and *c*. Later the court reconsiders the matter, rejects its earlier decisions as mistaken, and enlarges the interpretation of the statute to include act *d*. This second, expansive, interpretation will be held in the proper judicial forum to be unconstitutional, for it may penalize the man who conducted himself in accordance with the law as it was first interpreted by the courts themselves. All of these constitutional restraints express a determination to keep the criminal law free from the more obvious injustices that may result not only from retrospective statutes, but from the retrospective interpretation of statutes as well.

In concluding our somewhat lengthy treatment of the problem of retrospectivity it will be well to remind the reader again that this problem, like all the others presented by the common law, must be viewed as one aspect of an integrated system of institutional practices. If the common law were not developed out of cases as the accidents of litigation bring them up for decision – if, instead, the courts undertook to manage in advance the order in which legal issues were accepted for resolution, the problem of the retrospective effect of judicial determinations would bear a quite different aspect. Again, if judicial opinions were short, announced rules without reasons, and presented the facts in capsule form, it would be difficult to 'draw new law from the old books', or to fit judicial decisions into a coherent body of general principle, or to engage in the practice we have described as that of borrowing legal wisdom across political boundaries.

What has just been said makes it clear that any final appraisal of the common law, and any comparison of it with rival systems, must take into account the system as a whole. Each institutional practice bears a double aspect; seen in isolation it may appear to entail inconveniences and sometimes even injustices; seen as part of a larger unity it will partake of whatever virtues may properly be attributed to the system as a whole.

The complaint most frequently directed against the common law concerns the related faults of complexity and inaccessibility. Instead of being compacted in a code that can be held in one hand, its rules are spread out in haphazard order through thousands of volumes; even the indexes to the cases take up shelves of library space. Instead of presenting the finished labour of a commission of experts, the common law is the never-completed work of judges collaborating across generations and dealing with a great miscellany of disparate situations. Every rule of the common law carries on its back not only the reasons for it but often divergent articulations of those reasons, not to speak of recorded dissents and doubts or of tortured rationalizations, outright fictions, and other awkward manifestations of the effort to respect established precedent and yet keep the law in touch with a changing society.

A defence against these charges might run along the following lines: The unattractive qualities just described are the inevitable accompaniments of a legal system that develops its rules out of the decisions of actual controversies. The common law has the virtue that it inevitably mirrors the variety of human experience; it offers an honest reflection of the complexities and perplexities of life itself, instead of concealing them in the specious geometry of a code. In reality, codified law commonly offers a simplified pattern remote from the actual affairs of men. It deals with diagrammatically conceived situations which seldom correspond to actual cases. The result is that courts which 'apply' codified law build up an extensive 'common law' of their own, which suffers seriously from the fact that it pretends to be something it is not. It does not carry with it the burdens and doubts of its origins, and it cannot therefore – in the famous words of Lord Mansfield – 'work itself pure' by the process of comparison, re-examination, and re-articulation that characterizes the common law.

What has here been said of the common law makes it clear

that that system demands – and tends to develop – certain distinctive intellectual qualities. One can trace the influence of those qualities much beyond the courtroom, for they extend into legal education, the role of the legal profession, and even to styles in draftsmanship. It can safely be said that legal education in the common law countries has, over the years, displayed a greater intellectual vigour than can generally be found in the countries of the civil law. Those who have studied law on the Continent, for example, are astounded at how hard students work in American law schools. This surprise will express itself in such observations as, 'Why, your law students work as hard as our medical students do at home.' Though other cultural influences are no doubt operative, it is likely that a large part of this difference can be attributed to the fact that the common law arises out of the decision of actual cases, the facts of which are reported at length and studied closely. This lends a certain dramatic interest to the work of the classroom; one feels that one is in contact with the problems of real people. Even the figures of Lumley and Gye, those litigious rivals of the theatrical world of a London now faded into the historical past, become like old friends and certainly carry with them more of the sense of human flesh than the Primus and Secundus of the Roman sources.

More fundamentally, however, the special challenge of the common law lies in the fact that the articulation of its rules and the explanation of them – their 'grounding in principle' – represent tasks that are never finished. When a student is asked to state how a case should be decided he is expected to bring it into harmony not simply with some one-sentence generalization but with a body of law already showing the strains of its accommodation to a broken pattern of previous litigations, the decisions of which must be re-examined in the process of applying them to the case at hand. Nothing is more inhibitive in education than setting up a barrier beyond which questions of the 'why' become irrelevant; there is no better 'why-stopper' than codified law. To be sure, it is possible to go behind the statute to inquire whether it was soundly conceived and aptly phrased, but this involves a diversion of attention and requires a distinct effort of the will. What thus appears as a detour in the civil law is part of the main highway of the common law.

It would be invidious to attempt here any comparison of the quality of the human material that is attracted into the legal profession in the various countries. It is safe to say, however, that in the common law countries the profession plays a more active, participatory, and managerial role in affairs than it does generally elsewhere. A portion of this special quality may be attributed to the circumstances that the common law is itself constantly immersed in affairs; it draws its rules from cases that display all the entanglements into which human beings, well-meaning or otherwise, can get themselves. In the United States, before the rise of schools of business administration, it was common for young men planning careers in management to take a law degree. This practice was definitely not predicated on the assumption that this would enable them, as businessmen, to dispense with outside legal counsel. It was, instead, based on the assumption that the study of law by the case method was itself a valuable training for the handling of affairs. Certainly it is true that any student who has completed the first-year course in contracts has had his imagination sharpened for perceiving the ways in which carefully negotiated arrangements can miscarry and give rise to dispute between men of good intentions. This capacity is not without relevance to the discharge of managerial responsibilities, whether in the government or in business.

It is a common observation that distinct styles of draftsmanship can be discerned in lawyers trained in the two great legal traditions. Documents drafted by attorneys trained in the civil law tend to be short and abstract, after the pattern of a code. The common law style, on the other hand, runs to greater elaboration and a more strenuous effort to foresee possible contingencies; the draftsman attempts as best he can to eliminate the likelihood or need for litigation by resolving in advance any difficulties that may arise.

Whether the account just given – which could be greatly extended – is entirely apt or not, there can be no question that there is a noticeable difference in what may be called 'legal style' observable in lawyers trained in the two traditions. This is confirmed by the remark of a perceptive European lawyer who spent a year of study in the United States. During his visit this lawyer had devoted most of his time to a study of subjects directly relevant to his speciality, international law. At the end of the year, however, he remarked that if he were doing it over again he would devote most of his attention to the basic, fundamental subjects such as contracts, torts, and property, which are taught in the first year of law school. He explained that he had come to see that one of the most serious obstacles to understanding between lawyers trained in the two systems lay not in linguistic difficulties or varying conceptions of the subject matter under discussion, but in fundamental ways and habits of thought acquired in their basic legal training.

If our account were terminated at this point it would convey to the reader a quite one-sided view of the merits of the common law system. Those merits are genuine, but they are not to be realized simply by an application – anywhere and under all circumstances – of the institutional practices and modes of thought that compose the common law. That system is a specialized tool, apt for some uses and wholly unsuited to others. Unfortunately, appraisals generally do not take this aspect of the matter into consideration and tend, instead, to run toward extremes of general approval or disapproval. On the one hand, the common law may be seen as a kind of institutional fraud, resting on a superstitious awe of the judicial office peculiar to Anglo-American peoples; on the other hand, it may be depicted as a kind of legal cure-all, capable of healing all the ills of government and of creating a universal legal order.

In what follows we shall seek a more balanced judgement; we shall attempt to weigh, against merits already described at length, important limitations we have so far largely passed over in silence. We shall seek to demonstrate that the common law, or any system of adjudicative law patterned after that model, is not an apt instrument of social order in the following cases: 1) where the task is that of declaring what acts shall be treated as crimes; 2) where opinion in the society in question is deeply divided on issues affecting law, government, and economic organization; 3) in societies undergoing rapid and disruptive change; 4) where the task assigned for adjudicative solution may be described as being broadly 'managerial' in nature.

We have already reported that in the countries of the common law the whole of criminal law has now been largely entrusted to legislative regulation. The truth is that its criminal branch has never formed one of the proudest chapters in the common law. In this branch of the law a controlling consideration is to let everyone know where he stands, to inform him in advance as to what he can do and not do. This desideratum is poorly served by a system that grows case by case as problems are brought to court for solution.

It may be useful in this connection to compare the law of crimes with that of contracts. The latter branch of law serves the purpose of fostering and reinforcing a regime of order that grows up outside the courtroom and is capable of functioning in some degree without the aid of law. If our objective is to achieve an economic order based on free exchange, that order will, as it develops, tend to reveal in litigated cases the principles necessary to sustain it. Nothing like that can occur, of course, in the criminal law. Crime represents disorder and social entropy; the task of the law is to protect society against it. Though an effective discharge of that task requires an understanding of the causes of crime, that understanding is not likely to be attained through processes of adjudication.

Our observation that contract law reflects the principles essential for a regime of free exchange leads naturally to our next point: The common law can be expected to succeed only among peoples who share some common conception of the bases of social order. A system of adjudicative law operating without formal rules fixed in advance must, of necessity, draw much of its guidance from standards implicit in the social environment in which it functions. If that environment is such that it cannot furnish what might be called the raw stuff of law, then it is unsuited to regulation by the methods of the common law.

A trite way of phrasing the point just suggested would be to say that there must be enough agreement on general values within the society in question so that the judge, by deciding cases in accordance with those values, can be assured of general approval for his decisions. There are, however, two difficulties with this formulation. First, general values do not decide concrete issues, especially not those acute enough to give rise to litigation. Secondly, judicial decisions commonly relate to special situations of fact with which the population as a whole has no acquaintance and on which it would, therefore, have no occasion to form an opinion.

Instead of asking whether the state of public opinion is such that by conforming to it the judge can secure acceptance for his decisions, it would be better to ask whether it offers some assurance that the litigants in arguing their cases will be able to reach a meaningful joinder of issue. We must not forget that the process of adjudication has within itself a *social* dimension. We cannot define a judge simply as one who is bound to reach his decisions impartially; such a definition would not distinguish him from many others who exercise the powers of government. A judge is one who decides disputes within an institutional framework assuring to the litigant a collaborative role, which consists in the opportunity to state, prove, and argue his case. This participation of the affected party loses its point if the litigants talk past one another, so that all each says is irrelevant to the other's conception of the issues involved in their controversy.

Joinder of issue is, of course, a relative matter, and some lack of jibe between the litigants' contentions is not uncommon in any system of adjudication. Indeed, even under the most carefully drafted code it will sometimes happen that one litigant will base his case entirely on one section of the code, while his opponent will derive his arguments from a quite different provision. Yet with all allowance for this intrinsic risk, it is still true that if it became generally the case that the litigants could never join issue meaningfully, in any kind of litigation, then adjudication would forfeit its meaning as a distinctive process for achieving social order. Indeed, one may go further and suggest that the most reliable symptom of general social health is not agreement on vague 'general values', but lies in shared standards by which differences can be isolated, discussed meaningfully, and subjected ultimately to some rational resolution.

It is, in any event, this kind of consensus that is essential to the successful functioning of a system of adjudicative law that develops its rules of decision out of the process of the decision itself. On this basis it may be doubted whether the right route to international peace lies in creating a world court with the power to decide disputes among nations by standards to be worked out by the court itself as the cases come to decision. Before such a court could function successfully, a more meaningful community among nations would have to be achieved. The routes to this lie in increased communication and exchange, in the tacit accommodations out of which customary law is born, and, where it turns out to be possible, in explicit contractual arrangements in the form of treaties. The groundwork thus laid might at some future time furnish the substratum essential for an international common law.

The third limitation to which the common law is subject requires little discussion: It is a system badly suited to dealing with societies undergoing rapid change. Its leisurely methods of development unfit it for dealing with conditions of emergency. Certainly it should not be recommended to societies undergoing a forced industrialization or other drastic reorderings, such as that involved in a wholesale redistribution of land holdings.

Our final point is related to that just made: The methods of the common law are unsuited to what may broadly be called 'managerial' tasks. One cannot, through the adjudicative forms of the common law, accomplish, without a damaging distortion, such tasks as directing the operation of an airline, managing a hospital, or allocating railway facilities within a nation. In the case of a contract between A and the government, one can adjudicate which of the parties was right in a dispute about the terms of their agreement; one cannot adjudicate effectively the question whether in the future the government would be well-advised to place its contracts with A or B or C, or should perhaps undertake to manufacture the goods in question for itself.

It may be objected that this is too obvious a point to require demonstration and that, in any event, it relates to the forms of law generally and not simply to those characteristic of the common law. But this easy dismissal would ignore the lesson of history that the common law experience has in fact proved misleading. No one would suppose that if the government were concerned to exercise a directive power over some broad field of economic activity, it should first enact a comprehensive code of rules and then set up a special tribunal that, acting as a court, would interpret and apply the rules to the solution of specific problems. The flexible response to changing conditions characteristic of economic activity would preclude any such rule-bound administration. But the common law system seems to start without any rules at all, and then works out its principles of decision case by case as problems arise. This method of going about its task lends to that system a superficial resemblance to managerial activity. This has encouraged the belief that where the government undertakes to regulate and direct some area of the economy it can do this effectively by methods akin to those of the common law. Thus, an administrative tribunal may be created with essentially no instructions except that its decisions should be such as will 'promote the public interest'; the tribunal is then expected, acting through formal hearings patterned after court proceedings, to accomplish the needed regulation and direction.

There are many faults with the analogy on which this practice is based. Though the common law works out its rules case by case, in the end its decisions declare legal rights and duties; they do not say, as managerial directions must, 'Do thus and so until further notice.' Furthermore, the issues presented for resolution under the common law are of such a nature that the litigants themselves can normally understand, and have access to, the considerations relevant to the decision of the court. In complex economic activities, on the other hand, every part is in interaction with the whole; to obtain through adjudicative procedures all the information necessary for economic direction would overfill the hearing chamber with 'litigants', each with a different, segmental story of the relevance of a contemplated decision to his fractional participation in the whole undertaking. (It should be recalled that if the interested parties were in effect placed in line, so that each came in turn to tell his story in the absence of the others, an essential element of adjudication would be lost – that each litigant have a chance to know firsthand what the other has said so that he may comment effectively on it.)

In discussions of governmental policy the issue just suggested is often phrased in these terms: What functions of government should be 'judicialized', that is, discharged through processes patterned after those of a court of law? Probably the United States has gone further than any other country in this matter of 'judicialization'. In attempting to understand this phenomenon it should be observed that during the past half-century the common law has demonstrated in the United States a remarkable capacity for growth. What we are suggesting is that this success contains within it dangers, and it may already have led to an uncritical extension of judicial forms to governmental functions that cannot – without inefficiency and hypocrisy – be discharged through those forms.

Of necessity, the observations just concluded concerning the limitations of the common law system have been summary and at times elliptical. They will have accomplished their purpose if they have convinced the reader that there is a real problem in keeping the common law system in its proper place – a place where it is capable of functioning very well indeed.

A philosophic postscript – natural law and legal positivism

As we bring our account of the legal order to its close, it will be well to recall certain basic elements in our analysis. We have distinguished four distinct sources of legal rules: 1) legislative enactment, 2) explicit contract, 3) tacit accommodations of the sort that give rise to customary law, and 4) adjudication as it functions in the system that has come to be

known as the common law. In a loose sense these may be said
to present rival systems for the making of law. But from a
different point of view, which we have much emphasized, each
of these institutional forms subjects the law it 'makes' to a different set of influences, which we have designated as implicit
elements entering into the law that finally emerges.

When we first introduced the distinction between made law
and implicit law, we noted in passing that this distinction had
more than a superficial relation to an ancient debate among
legal philosophers: that which separates the 'legal positivists'
from the advocates of 'natural law'. It is now time to re-
examine this affinity in somewhat greater depth. To define just
what it means to be an adherent of natural law is a difficult
undertaking. We shall, accordingly, start with the somewhat
easier task of describing what is meant by legal positivism.

It will not be far off the mark to say of the legal positivist
that he is an apostle of made law. In a phrase we have previously used, he is one with a strong preference for the intellectual flavour of made law. This preference manifests itself
in many ways. It comes to expression, for example, in the
repeated assertion that the judges of the common law make law
just as surely as do legislative assemblies. In a sense, of course,
this is true, but insistence on it without qualification conveys
the mistaken notion – which is in fact generally shared by adherents of legal positivism – that it is safe to ignore differences
in the institutional procedures by which these two agencies
'make' their law.

Again, a distrust of implicit elements in law and lawmaking
leads Austin to deny the quality of law to customary rules
until they have been stamped with the imprimatur of the state,
until – in other words – they have been 'remade' by the state.
We have previously* attempted to show how this construction
distorts and simplifies the facts.

Another illustration of the same inclination of the mind is
found in Gray's *Nature and Sources of the Law*. In Chapter 4
of that work Gray raises the question whether there can be
said to be any 'law' on a question which has 'never arisen . . .

* See pp. 65–8.

before' in a jurisdiction and where there is 'no statute, no decision, [and] no custom' affecting the matter. He concludes that in such a situation there is no law on the issue in question at all; it confronts, as it were, a legal vacuum. On one interpretation this proposition is true, but a tautology; it simply asserts, 'I so define law that there can be no law within a jurisdiction until there is something there that meets my definition of law.' But if Gray meant to say that in the situation he supposes there could be no possible way of anticipating how a court would decide a novel case, he is plainly mistaken.

Within any society there are contentions which run so counter to generally shared assumptions that they would be rejected out of hand by any judge of sound mind. A man kills his father; in answer to a charge of murder he pleads that his father was a virtuous man with a firm belief in heaven; the taking of his life, therefore, dispatched him into an infinity of happiness such as he could never enjoy on earth; one who confers such a boon should be rewarded, not punished. An official embezzles a large sum from the state; he answers the charge against him by citing a preamble of the constitution declaring that the state exists to promote the greatest happiness of the greatest number; the money he took made the defendant very happy; the resulting infinitesimal diminution in the wealth of every other citizen could not possibly produce a perceptible decrease in *his* happiness. (If these illustrations seem out of place in a serious context like the present, it may be remarked that St Thomas Aquinas dealt at some length with the problem of the first; Jeremy Bentham gave earnest attention to the issues presented by the second.)

Contentions like those just suggested are not ruled out of order by any statute, judicial decision, or custom. Their rejection does not depend on law; on the contrary, it may be said that the law depends on their rejection in the form of ordinary lay opinion. Some extralegal consensus on what is clearly out of bounds is essential to shrink the periphery of explicit law to workable dimensions. Paradoxically, the positivist who insists that all true law is explicitly made is the beneficiary of this silent exclusion; without it his 'law' would become too chaotic a thing to offer any anchorage for his faith.

At this juncture it will be helpful to offer some comparisons between legal positivism and its counterpart in science. Scientific positivism condemns any inquiry projecting itself beyond observable phenomena; it abjures metaphysics, it renounces in advance any explanation in terms of ultimate causes. Its programme of research is to chart the regularities discernible in the phenomena of nature at the point where they become open to human observation, without asking – as it were – how they got there. In the setting of limits to inquiry there is an obvious parallel between scientific and legal positivism. The legal positivist concentrates his attention on law at the point where it emerges from the institutional processes that brought it into being. It is the finally made law itself that furnishes the subject of his inquiries. How it was made and what directions of human effort went into its creation are for him irrelevancies.

The two kinds of positivism not only display a parallel in their beliefs but also in the difficulties they encounter in maintaining those beliefs. The scientific positivist runs into trouble in defining the barrier beyond which inquiry should not attempt to penetrate. 'Metaphysics' and other terms that may be applied in a pejorative sense have a certain polemic utility, but unfortunately they do not draw plain boundaries. The philosopher Morris Cohen used to say that metaphysics simply represents an attempt of the human mind to push as far into reality as it can. Among the positivists of scientific method there is, in fact, much difference of opinion as to when forbidden territory is entered. The injunction, 'Stick to observables', may encounter embarrassment; some of the greatest discoveries of science have come about by postulating structures or mechanisms that were not yet open to direct observation, some of them still remaining in that condition. In the midst of the debate about this and other issues, the practising scientist goes about his business, employing any and every useful means or dodge he can conceive or discover that will help him make sense of the facts as he perceives them.

The perplexities of knowing where to draw the line also

plague legal positivism. Customary law presents these perplexities at their maximum. When does customary law 'exist'? When have the reciprocal expectations that give rise to customary law become so firmly fixed that it becomes appropriate to regard them as creating obligations? When one reflects on the difficulty of answering these questions it becomes apparent why legal positivism tends to shun customary law, or, following Austin, converts it into a form of law more tractable to its philosophy. Subjecting the common law to a positivistic analysis presents difficulties not unlike those presented by customary law; the 'emergent' nature of its rules tends to make them resistant to the demands of a positivistic conception. It is only with legislatively enacted law that positivism feels itself reasonably at home, and that only – as we shall shortly see – so long as problems of interpretation are avoided.

The similarities displayed by legal positivism and its counterpart in science should not be allowed to obscure a crucial difference between the two. The scientific positivist can rest on one principle of exclusion that receives acceptance in the whole of modern science: Purpose is unacceptable as an explanation for the behaviour of inanimate matter (no one today would think of explaining the fall of a stone by saying that it is moved by an impulse to rejoin its mother, Earth). Legal positivism cannot accomplish this exclusion so comfortably. Law is a product of human effort, and we risk absurdity if we try to describe it in disregard of what those who brought it into being were trying to do.

This difference between scientific and legal positivism becomes most clear when we consider the badly conceived or defectively drafted law. Inanimate nature does not make mistakes; legislators do. A meteor or molecule cannot miss its mark; a statute can. There are numerous ways in which a law can go wrong in terms of its own objectives: it can fail in its basic structure, in the details of its wording, in its conception of the factual situation towards which it was directed, and in many other ways. A judge charged with the responsibility of applying a statute must often face the question of how far he is at liberty to correct its mistakes. He may feel free to rectify

a text suffering from an obvious misprint; he is not likely to
consider that his office entitles him to redraft a whole enactment to make it a more effective instrument for achieving its
aim. Between these extremes he faces difficult problems of
judgment, problems which positivism cannot help him solve,
since their very existence is inconsistent with the premises of
the philosophy.

The problem of the statute defective in terms of its own
objective simply brings to the surface the difficulties that problems of interpretation generally are bound to present to a
philosophy that attempts to sever law from its sources. The
proper interpretation of laws constitutes one of the most vital
concerns of lawyers and judges, yet it is one on which positivism
has almost nothing to say. In practice, legal positivists tend to
ignore such problems either by passing over them in silence
or by dismissing them as belonging not strictly to the law at
all but to politics, sociology, and ethics. Where interpretation
is discussed in the literature of positivism, there is generally
revealed an assumption that in most cases a statute can be
applied simply by reading its words without considering its
purpose or function; a reference to the purpose of the statute
becomes necessary, it is assumed, only in an occasional and
exceptional case. In reality, the statute so plain in meaning
that it seems to require no interpretation at all owes its clarity
not to the dictionary meaning of its words, but to the fact that
its purpose is so clear and familiar that any reasonably intelligent citizen can see what it is attempting to accomplish.

Let us turn now to what is generally regarded as the opposite
of legal positivism: the theory of natural law. We have previously observed that it is not easy to say what it means to be
an adherent of natural law. It is, however, a relatively simple
task to combine in one package all the dogmatisms that have
been attributed to – and have sometimes been exemplified in –
the philosophy of natural law. Thus relieved of caution and discharged of any responsibility to be sensible, the philosophy of
natural law would embrace the following beliefs: There is an
ideal system of law dictated by God, by the nature of man, or
by nature itself. This ideal system is the same for all societies

and for all periods of history. Its rules can be discerned by reason and reflection. Enacted laws that run counter to this ideal law are void and can make no moral claim to be obeyed.

It is easy to refute these affirmations. The laws of a preliterate society will inevitably and properly differ from those of a nation where every adult citizen can read and abundant resources are available for communication by the printed word. The legal systems appropriate for countries where water is scarce will necessarily differ from those suited to lands of abundant rainfall; among other points of difference, the legal systems of the first class will confront the necessity of dealing with recurrent crises caused by drought; the legal institutions of the second will not be subjected to this strain. Other considerations of climate, geography, technology, culture, and past history have to be taken into account in the design of any legal system. Even if all these factors could be assigned their proper weight, the demands of natural law could still never be capable of anything like a geometric demonstration. If every citizen reserved to himself a private veto over enacted law that in his opinion violated the law of nature, we would indeed, in Bentham's words, be in for 'a cut-throat time of it'.

Rejecting, then, the dogmatisms often associated with the theory of natural law, let us move to the opposite end of the scale of affirmation and present that theory as it might appear in its most modest form. Its fundamental tenet is an affirmation of the role of human reason in the design and operation of legal institutions. It asserts that there are principles of sound social architecture, objectively given, and that these principles, like those of physical architecture, do not change with every shift in the details of the design towards which they are directed. Those who participate in the enterprise of law must acquire a sense of institutional role and give thought to how that role may most effectively be discharged without transcending its essential restraints. All of these are matters of perception and understanding and need not simply reflect personal predilection or inherited tradition.

If the virtue of the natural law theory has been to keep alive faith in the capacity of human reason, its vice has often been to overstate the role rationality can play in human affairs. Reason can shape the fundamental structure of a legal system; it cannot prepare the law to deal with every twist and turn that human affairs can take. Under any legal system embarrassing and borderline cases will arise that can, with equal rationality or irrationality, be decided either way. To reach some disposition of these cases we must employ a principle of authoritative decision and pass them over to a judge or administrator to decide, not because he will know how to decide them, but simply because somebody must. Legislative foresight can reduce the number of such cases, but it can never entirely eliminate them.

A too ardent faith in the theory of natural law may not only leave us unprepared for peripheral uncertainties of the sort just described, but may also distort our conception of problems affecting the fundamental structure of a legal order. In our analysis we have distinguished four kinds of law: legislative enactment, customary law, contractual law, and adjudicative law as exemplified in the common law system. Now each of these forms of law has its virtues and defects; in dealing with a given area of human life it is often possible to demonstrate with some persuasiveness that one form is a more apt instrument of social order than the others. Yet there is a strong tendency to arrange them along a scale of relative 'rationality'. In such a ranking, legislative enactment and explicit contract are apt to share first place, while customary law will be assigned to the bottom. In a sense this ranking is justified; legislation and contract *are* more 'rational' than customary law precisely because they presuppose and require a more effective communication among those concerned with them. But what shall we do when the ordinary forms of communication become difficult or break down entirely? Then the silent reciprocal adjustments that go into the making of customary law come into their own. They must not be dismissed because they are 'primitive' if the situation to which they are applied is itself 'primitive'.

It is scarcely necessary to remind the reader that the comments just made have a considerable relevance to a world in

which great and powerful nations are divided into hostile
groups, groups between which communication is at best imperfect. A mind taken up with grandiose pictures of an ideal world
order may well view with disdain the most effective means by
which the gap of understanding can be narrowed, that is, by
the tacit, face-saving accommodations that give rise to customary law. When that law has become extensive enough and
has taken a sufficiently firm grip, then it can perhaps be displaced by more 'advance' forms of law: broad treaties, international legislation, and, eventually perhaps, adjudication by a
world court with compulsory jurisdiction.

Can there be some as yet unformulated ideal system, standing above the familiar expressions of law, in incorporating in
itself all their virtues and none of their defects? It is difficult
to conceive what it would be. An impatient quest for the ultimate in rationality might suggest an attack along these lines:
Since each of the distinctive forms of law is like a specialized
tool, apt for some uses and less suited to others, why not apply
each form to those situations where it is demonstrably most
effective? Why not preserve flexibility by fitting the forms of
law directly to the demands of life, instead of deploying them
after an irregular pattern set by the accidents of history and
the unplanned configurations of society itself?

Any such attempt would inevitably miscarry, even at the
stage of intellectual formulation. The analogy of language can
serve to reveal why this must be so. One might conceive of an
ideal language as one capable of arranging the raw material
of experience into an infinity of patterns, each capable of
depicting some special aspect of reality that happened to be
of interest at the moment. But such an impossibly flexible
language would forfeit its fundamental function: communication. Communication demands firm base lines and shared expectations. This means that the distinctions which a given language can express must be limited in number. It may be said of
the basic forms of a language that they always reveal one relationship at the cost of obscuring another. It is, for example,
hard to conceive of a language without something like the distinction between nouns and verbs. Yet nouns tend to reify pro-

cesses and convert them into static things; the transitive verb obscures interaction and reciprocal influence – by telling us that A acts on B, it makes us forget that in the process A is altered by its contact with B. Anyone familiar with the problems of translation knows that the forms of a language which show it to good advantage in one context may become an impediment to clear and graceful expression in another.

It is not otherwise with systems of law. Legal forms cannot be fitted plastically to new situations as they arise; they must extend over readily understood areas even at some sacrifice of aptness in individual cases. This means that in the design of a functioning legal system something like an accounting of relative costs is inevitable. The basic rationality of law cannot be that of logic or geometry; it must be like that of an economic calculation – 'all things considered, and weighing costs against advantages, X is better than Y'. The adherent of the theory of natural law may find this an unacceptable compromise. If so, perhaps his theory has failed to seek out sufficiently the natural laws to which human lawmaking is itself subject.

In the account we have given here we have made no attempt to describe, or even to suggest, all the permutations to which the philosophies of legal positivism and natural law have historically been subject. Sometimes positivism moves towards a more ambitious end, that of reducing all human behaviour to forms of analysis taken from the sciences of inanimate matter; commonly adherents of legal positivism do not go so far. Though the philosophy of natural law has always rested on a faith in reason, sometimes the reason required is thought to exceed human capacity and to be attainable only through revelation. We have here depicted the theory of natural law in what might be called its revolutionary or ameliorative aspect, though its rhetoric has sometimes been employed to sustain the status quo by asserting that the existing law itself expresses the law of nature. In this employment there tends to be a very considerable vagueness about the model by which existing law is vindicated; too great particularity on that score, by furnishing a standard for change, could easily disserve the cause of quietism.

With all their flexibility, and the permutations to which they have been subject historically, it is unlikely that the opposition between the two schools will ever entirely disappear. They bring to expression a fundamental polarity. The one school emphasizes what is fixed and given in the law; it counsels us to view law for what it is, instead of interpreting it after our notions of the end towards which it is or should be striving. The other school reminds us that the given law, viewed through time, is inevitably in development and the direction of its development lies in part with the viewer since he is a participant in setting that direction. Since at particular junctures in human affairs both kinds of counsel can seem pertinent, it is likely that both kinds will continue to be offered in the future.

Index

More about Penguins and Pelicans

Penguinews, which appears every month, contains details of all the new books issued by Penguins as they are published. From time to time it is supplemented by *Penguins in Print*, which is a complete list of all available books published by Penguins. (There are well over three thousand of these.)

A specimen copy of *Penguinews* will be sent to you free on request, and you can become a subscriber for the price of the postage. For a year's issues (including the complete lists) please send 30p if you live in the United Kingdom, or 60p if you live elsewhere. Just write to Dept EP, Penguin Books Ltd, Harmondsworth, Middlesex, enclosing a cheque or postal order, and your name will be added to the mailing list.

Note: *Penguinews* and *Penguins in Print* are not available in the U.S.A. or Canada

A Penguin Special

Civil Liberty: The N.C.C.L. Guide

Anna Coote

No constitution or charter protects British rights. At the
mercy of any piece of hasty or prejudiced legislation, they
must be upheld in every generation.

Do you possess the 'eternal vigilance' required to safeguard
liberty? Do you know, for instance, what your rights are if
you are arrested; if you want to hold a meeting or a lottery;
to demonstrate in public or vote or strike; to eject an
unwelcome visitor or evict a tenant; to adopt a baby or get
a divorce; to be educated or obtain a council house or a
supplementary benefit; to park your car or sue your dentist?

If you are unsure, this Penguin Special will supply the
answers. You will find detailed here all those questions of
liberty, justice and human rights about which most men in
in the street are ignorant or, at best, doubtful. In effect this
well ordered and useful guide distils the long experience of the
National Council of Civil Liberties in standing up (both
politically and through case-work) for 'us' against 'them'.